"Finally, a sound, well-written book about a univei
neglected subject."

—M. Scott Peck, M.D., author o
Traveled and *In Search of Stone*

"This wise and greatly needed book offers concern
helpful insights, inspiring stories, and practical tools for
boundaries, being supportive without meddling, and de
communication with their adult children."

—Christine Evans, author of *Bro
Shame Trap

"This is a subject that conscientious parents of grov
agonize over. Most of us need some guidance in this diff
crucial area."

—Robert Pierpoint, CBS News (
(retired)

"If you worry about your grown children, this is a
turn to instead of Mylanta. Its most basic lesson: you aren't alone. It
tells how other parents are dealing with exactly the same transient or
tragic situations, provides practical exercises that help you understand
yourself better, and, with a wide range of quotes, gives a glimpse of the
enduring values that underlie the day-to-day confusion of parenthood.
It may also remind you—the best lesson of all—what great kids you
have."

—Reg Green, Nicholas Green Foundation

BECOMING A

WISE
PARENT

GROWN
CHILD

How to Give Love and Support
Without Meddling

**BETTY FRAIN, PH. D.,
& EILEEN M. CLEGG**

New Harbinger Publications, Inc.

The quoted material on pages 7, 49, and 65 is reprinted by permission of the author and publisher of *The New Peoplemaking*, Virginia Satir. 1972. Palo Alto, CA: Science and Behavior Books, Inc. 1-800-547-9982

Publisher's Note

Distributed in the U.S.A. by Publishers Group West; in Canada by Raincoast Books; in Great Britain by Airlift Book Company, Ltd.; in South Africa by Real Books, Ltd.; in Australia by Boobook; and in New Zealand by Tandem Press.

Cover design by Blue Design
Edited by Kayla Sussell and Angela Watrous
Typeset by Michele Waters

Library of Congress Catalog Card Number: 97-66075
ISBN 1-57224-081-4 Paperback

Printed in Canada on recycled paper.

New Harbinger Publications' Web site address: www.newharbinger.com

First Edition

This book is dedicated to
Iris Ridgway,
who inspired the work.

Contents

Foreword

In my fifty-year career in medicine—as a country general practitioner and later as a medical school professor—I came to understand a great deal about the complexities of family dynamics and the healing potential of parental love in the lives of my patients. But these days I am understanding those lessons on a more personal level.

During the past twelve years, I have been attending behavior modification sessions to change me from a rushed, controlling, aggressive personality to a relaxed, lovable old man. But just a couple of years ago, my wife, Mary, warned me to quit being overly critical. "Stop trying to control what your kids do or they'll never want to see you," she said. I thought, "After all, I'm their father and I love them. Why shouldn't I tell them if I think they're too fat, drinking too much, living with too much tension, or in need of some advice about marriage and childrearing?"

Eileen Clegg asked me to write the foreword for this book at a time when I was gathered with my family for a big event—ceremonies honoring my number three son, Dr. Jon Kim Andrus, who received the 1997 Alumnus Humanitarian Award from his alma mater, The University of California, Davis, School of Medicine. I was awash with great pride in his accomplishments, just as my father felt proud of me for following in his footsteps as a physician. All four of my children, and ten of my grandchildren, gathered together for this event. I basked in the glow of this wonderful assemblage of my gene pool. I am proud of all my children and grandchildren. It was a hectic time, but as it turned out, a fortuitous time, to find in my hands the manuscript *Becoming a Wise Parent for Your Grown Child.*

I read the book with my ex-wife, Kathleen, the mother of our four children, and together we did some of the exercises. We laughed a lot and cried some. In this last chapter of our lives, we are struggling not to "meddle" in our children's lives, but to enjoy them and offer them unconditional love. As Kathleen and I went over the exercises, we reviewed our family relationships—the dynamics we experienced with our own parents, their strong and their weak points. We both could see how our parenting related to how we were parented. I thought of my difficult relationship with my own father and felt sad because we never healed the wounds that we inflicted on each other. I am sure that the ideas expressed in this book would have helped our relationship, if we had been able to read them. I am in the process of reconsidering some of my judgmental ways in favor of a more supportive and less intrusive role. Stick with me, kids!

Eileen and Betty: Your book will be helpful to any parent, old ones like I am or young ones like you are. If we can practice what this book teaches and combine it with unconditional love, the world will become a better place. Maybe we can stop some of the harmful parenting habits that are passed from generation to generation.

—LEN HUGHES ANDRUS, M.D.,
Professor Emeritus, University
of California, Davis, School of
Medicine

Introduction

I'll love you forever, I'll like you for always,
As long as I'm living, my baby you'll be.

—Robert Munsch, *Love You Forever*
(children's book)

Parental love may endure forever, but the ability to express that love can become painfully stifled when children enter adulthood. Even though parents may yearn to play a joyful and supportive part in the lives of their grown-up kids, they often are confused about their parental roles, and justifiably.

Just think for a moment about the term most often used to describe the act of participating in an adult child's life—"meddling." It's a nasty thud of a word, seemingly designed to engender shame. Who wants to be known as *meddlesome*? It invokes images of a shrewish person prying into other people's business while the fifties' song "Mother-in-Law" plays in the background.

The fear of finding yourself transformed into such a creature is almost enough to keep concerns about your grown children locked away in a private place. One day, perhaps, the stigma will lift and people in midlife will feel free to talk with one another honestly about the joys and sorrows that naturally occur in relationships with their adult offspring.

This book is offered as an interim measure. It presents some intimate glimpses into the different kinds of challenges faced by conscientious parents of grown children today and provides a supportive, step-by-step process for working through some of those challenges. Just as child development books helped you deal with the issues that came up when your youngsters were growing, this book offers you a new set of tools for becoming an effective parent now that they're adults.

There's a fine line between sharing wisdom and meddling, and there are few guideposts for finding that line. Traditional rules that used to govern intergenerational relationships have changed. As a result, adult children need loving support from their parents more than ever in our increasingly complex society. Love is the beginning, but sometimes love isn't enough to sustain relationships when delicate moral issues arise, or when parents are troubled by the paths their children choose. It takes creativity, self-awareness, and often a saintlike tolerance for ambiguity if parents are to maintain healthy relationships with their grown kids.

If you've ever shrugged your shoulders or rolled your eyes in utter exasperation over how to handle certain situations, you are not alone. More and more often, psychologists find themselves counseling people who are not seeking therapy for their own problems, but rather guidance in how to help their adult children deal with complex issues.

Among the questions these parents ask are these:

- How do I share my wisdom without giving unwanted advice?

- How can I feel closer to my grown children?

- How can I make the most out of family gatherings?

- How can I learn to listen without being judgmental?

- How can I tell the difference between healthy interdependence and unhealthy codependence in a close relationship with my adult child?

- How can I offer assistance without undermining my child's autonomy?

- When I see my child treat their child in a way that I know to be damaging, should I speak up, keep quiet, or talk privately with my grandchild?

- How can I start discussions with my children about my concerns about my growing older?

- What's the key to giving feedback without sounding overly critical?

- What's the best way to offer financial assistance to my grown children without thwarting their need to become responsible with money and without compromising my own financial stability?

- How am I supposed to respond when my adult children blame my parenting techniques for the problems they're experiencing as adults?

- How can I become more involved with my grandchildren?

- How can I retain a close relationship with my grandchildren without my children coming to depend upon me for child care?

- If I sense that my adult children are in dangerous situations—such as dealing with domestic abuse or substance addictions—should I step in, even if they are not open to making changes?

- How do I relate to my grown child who has chosen a lifestyle radically different from my own?

Most caring parents with grown kids could contribute several more questions to this list, along with a skyward look and the age-old lamentation: "I would do the right thing if only I could figure out what it is."

It's often more difficult to find answers about how to help with your grown children's challenges than it was to cope with the problems they had when they were younger. Parents of small children can rely on family traditions and long talks with other parents at school functions and other children's events to help them deal with the day-to-day issues that arise. Parents of grown kids are more likely to find themselves looking for clues about what to do because they don't have as many conversations with other parents. Furthermore, they may not even know what their kids' day-to-day lives are really like.

There are several other reasons why parenting adults is more difficult than parenting young children. First of all, many parents feel ashamed if their grown children have problems. Parents may feel like failures if their children are not well-adjusted adults by age eighteen. Many books for parents imply that adolescence is the parents' last chance to be guiding and supportive influences in their children's lives. If you're overcome with guilt, it's hard to mobilize yourself to work on a mutually beneficial relationship with your grown child. Second, fewer resources are available on the emotional stages of adulthood than there are on the subject of child development. A parent is much more likely to know all about the "terrible two's" than the "busy thirties." So we tend to be unprepared for the normal ebb and flow that takes place in relationships with grown kids. Finally, many people are facing the fact that our society's definition of "normal" is changing so fast that the traditional roles of the parent-adult child relationship need to be redefined.

Fortunately, there are proven techniques for breaking down the barriers that stand in the way of parents who want to maintain a healthy influence in the lives of their children and grandchildren. Rather than relying on the old parenting model of helping children "solve their problems," this book offers you a new model for the fully functioning, multigenerational family that views problems as shared challenges. Grown children are blessed when they have a parent willing to invest the energy and take the risks necessary to deepen relationships with them. Parents who pick up this book are likely to be loving, proactive people who want to maximize their their personal growth and deepen their relationships.

In the following pages, you will be called upon to make an honest assessment of yourself, as a person and as a parent. You will have an opportunity to take a more objective look at the important role you can play in healing your family's past and guiding its future. As you gain insight into the issues affecting your child's life, this book will assist you in developing a strategy for becoming an effective supporter of your child. Once you recognize and appreciate your unique role in your family, you will find new and meaningful ways to contribute to the well-being of your adult children and to all the generations that follow.

How to Use This Book

Both an informational and interactive tool, this book is designed to allow you to learn more about yourself by doing the exercises in each chapter. Ideally, you will use this book as a notebook for recording responses to the exercises, along with insights and memories that are likely to emerge in the process. This notebook may one day become a treasure, a record of the creative effort that a loving parent invested toward the goal of strengthening family ties.

Many of the stories and topics covered in this book will be different from those affecting the lives of individual readers; however, the ideas and exercises apply to most parents. Even the best parents will find new ways to connect with their grown children. Readers facing immediate crises may "skip ahead" to chapters dealing with their particular issues. However, it's wise to do the introspective work suggested throughout the book while simultaneously taking the necessary steps to deal with a crisis.

Authors' Note

This book is designed to assist parents in the enrichment of relationships and mending of difficulties with their grown children. The ideas and exercises described here have helped many families, but they are not presented as substitutes for therapy or expert intervention. People dealing with psychiatric disorders or emotional instability, or taking medication for these problems, should consult a qualified mental health professional before proceeding with this material.

The stories in this book represent the factual unfolding of complex issues between parents and their grown children. The characters in this book are composites, based on family histories in which all names and identifying characteristics have been changed. Any resemblance to persons living or dead is purely coincidental.

Cast of Characters

Anne, who is concerned about the way her daughter nags Anne's grandson.

Beth, whose only son seeems to be drifting slowly out of her life because of pressure from his wife.

Connie, who is worried that her son may suffer from undiagnosed depression.

Don, whose lesbian daughter has a baby son; Don wants to be an influence on the boy, but his daughter is keeping her distance.

Jake, whose daughter is inexplicably rebuffing his long time plans to move closer to her family for his retirement years.

Kathryn, who believes that her son-in-law is cheating on her seemingly unaware daughter.

Lynn, whose forty-three-year-old son has an alcohol problem and has turned to his mother, again, for a place to live and financial and legal support.

Mark, who detects signs of physical and emotional abuse in his daughter's family.

Michael, who is disturbed by his son's spoiling of the grandchildren.

Paula, who wants to help her children lead happier, healthier lives with time-management, nutrition, and budgeting advice.

Richard, who loves his grandchildren but has grown weary of constant requests to provide child care.

Rosa, whose daughter often insults her with hostile remarks.

Sally, who is worried about her daughter's plans to marry a man who looks like a real loser.

Tom, whose twenty-four-year-old daughter wants to move home just at the time when he most needs his freedom from family responsibility.

CHAPTER 1

Becoming Healthier Families

To me, this is the end point of the bringing up of children—that they become autonomous, independent, creative people who are now peers to the people who introduced them into the world.

—Virginia Satir, *The New Peoplemaking*

The Sanscrit symbol is the same for "intimacy" and "enlightenment."

We want to see our grown children become self-reliant, content, and happy in their relationships. We'd like to experience a sense of joy in their presence. We want family gatherings to be occasions for celebration, humor, and comfort, rather than times of obligation, confusion, or tension. We all want to love and be loved for who we are.

In healthy parent-adult child relationships maturity brings an opportunity for a kind of in-depth mutual understanding that is irreplaceable. The shared history between you and your children means you don't need to do as much explaining. You have memories in common, you know a lot of the same people, and you may laugh at the same kind of jokes. You share stories, traditions, and heritage. What richer opportunity is there for humor and warmth? Just the touch of a hand, a telling word, or a teasing smile can go straight to the heart and bring on a flood of memories that you both share.

In this ideal scenario, grown children respect their parents' judgments and seek their counsel; the children are mature enough to recognize that they can learn from someone with more experience and are confident enough to accept suggestions without becoming defensive. At the same time, parents respect their children's choices, even if they would have chosen differently.

Stop for a moment to think about the possibilities. Picture your grown child in your mind and imagine a conversation where you both are feeling trust, compassion, and care, and are honest with each other. You are peers in the sense of feeling equal to one another, although your connection will always have the qualities unique to the parent-child relationship. You are healthy as autonomous individuals and yet comfortable with belonging to one another. You're realistic about one another, and you're clear about your limits. You don't feel responsible for each other, and yet you can count on one another in emergencies. When one of you says, "What can I do to help?" both the question and the answer come from an honest and loving place. You are refuges for one another in a tough world.

Healthy Does Not Mean Perfect

If the subject were more acceptable for casual conversation, you'd probably discover that, even in seemingly ideal families, most parents face troublesome issues involving their grown children at one time or another. There's the joke that "a dysfunctional family is a family with more than one person." While that's a stretch, it does hint at the truth: Any family with more than one person is bound to have problems at one time or another, ranging from irksome conflicts to shattering personal crises.

What separates healthy families from unhealthy families is not whether they have problems but how they handle them. Healthy families cherish their bonds, so they pay attention to anything that strains or threatens their relationships. They want to keep their loving bonds intact. Conscientious parents recognize that they almost always have something to offer to their grown-up children. According to Dr. Bernie Siegel, physician and author (1997), it has been proven that parental love is healing. "While you're at Harvard, they ask you to describe your parents. Thirty-five years later, they look you up. If you described your parents as friendly and loving parents, only 27 or 28 percent had suffered major diagnostic illness. If you described your parents in negative terms as unloving, 95 percent had suffered some major illness in that period."

Most parents are aware of the pivotal role they play in their young children's lives, but they may not recognize the meaningful part they can play in their grown children's lives. Even those parents who disappointed their children earlier in life can turn around and become positive influences. There are adults whose parents belatedly found a way to make an authentic connection and thereby transformed all of their lives with love. There are also some very sad people whose parents could not, or would not, stand by them during difficult times. When troublesome issues arise, one can either turn away or see the problem as an opportunity to demonstrate the enduring quality of parental love.

The book's composite characters, whose stories we will follow throughout the book, are among those who chose the loving path. As you embark on your own journey toward a more loving connection with your grown child, you'll share with these characters an intimate view of the unexpected changes and growth that transformed their lives and relationships.

Beth

It was "just you and me," cozy and pleasant, when Beth was a single mom raising her only son. Now he's twenty-five, married, and living 300 miles away. Beth treasures her time with him, but a growing coolness on the part of her daughter-in-law makes family get-togethers increasingly awkward and less frequent. Beth longs for more closeness but doesn't know how to approach the subject with her son.

Jake

"After I finally retire, your mom and I will move out to be close to you guys," Jake would say when he visited his daughter and her family in a neighboring state. They responded with enthusiasm in past years, but now that retirement time has come, Jake's daughter treats the subject of her parents' move almost like a joke and avoids discussion about the details. Jake needs clarification so he can plan the move, but he's afraid that an honest conversation with his daughter may result in her rejecting him.

Paula

Paula raised three kids while working full-time. Her expertise in juggling a career and a smooth-running household was hard-earned. Now that her kids are grown and facing similar challenges, she feels they could use some help with budgeting, nutrition, and time management. Paula wants to help, but she doesn't want to appear intrusive.

Sally

Sally's daughter is completing college with definite career plans, but she plans to marry an unambitious man who works at a fast-food restaurant. To Sally, he doesn't seem good enough to marry her daughter. Sally realizes she could alienate her daughter by speaking up, but feels she cannot stand by silently and let this marriage happen.

Connie

Outwardly, Connie's thirty-two-year-old son pretends he has his life together, despite a difficult divorce, but he hasn't been himself for the past few weeks. He says he's fine, but Connie finds herself reading articles about depression and seeing descriptions of her son in them. Connie does not want to insult her son, but feels she must find a way to help him.

Tom

Tom and his wife are planning to sell the house where they raised their three children so they can downsize their living quarters and travel. Now their twenty-four-year-old daughter wants to move home so she can afford to go back to school. Tom worries about rejecting his daughter, but he also is concerned about his own future.

Richard

Richard and his wife treasure their grandchildren and love spending time with them, but almost daily requests for child care are disrupting their other activities. Richard would be devastated if a frank discussion with his son resulted in a loss of closeness in the family, but he would like more control over scheduling visits with the grandkids.

Kathryn

Kathryn's son-in-law is a flagrant flirt. His wandering eye seems to be looking for more than harmless fun. He may be cheating, but Kathryn's daughter seems oblivious. Kathryn's urge is to protect her daughter but she is not sure if that means being honest or keeping quiet.

Michael

Michael's grandchildren have every conceivable toy, closets full of sports equipment, and brand-name clothing, but they do not appear to appreciate all they have, nor do they have any responsibilities at home. Michael believes his grandkids will grow up to be obnoxious brats if someone doesn't demand better behavior from them, but wonders if saying that is a grandfather's place.

Mark

Mark is worried that his son-in-law's discipline is too harsh. He wonders if his grandson and daughter are subject to abusive treatment. Mark feels driven to rescue his daughter but doesn't want to risk her withdrawing from him to save her marriage.

Anne

Anne's daughter is a good mom, but she sometimes nags her son to the point where he seems overly upset at the prospect of doing the simplest activities. Anne wants to discuss the situation with her daughter but wonders if it's appropriate to intervene in her daughter's parenting.

Lynn

Lynn's forty-three-year-old son has been involved in a drunk driving accident and wants his mother's financial support. He needs money for the court case that has resulted from his accident. Lynn is wary because he has a bad temper and fails to take responsibility for his actions. Now that he's in trouble, he expects Lynn to let him live with her and to drive him everywhere, since his license has been revoked. Lynn wants to help him, but not at the expense of wasting her own life.

Rosa

Rosa's daughter is a successful businesswoman, mother, and wife who turned her life around after a difficult adolescence, but she continues her teenage style of relating to Rosa with put-downs and insults. Rosa is afraid that if she speaks up then she may lose her daughter altogether, but she does not want to stand by and accept verbal abuse.

Don

Don has gone through some major adjustments to accept that his daughter is lesbian and to ensure that she and her partner feel part of the family. Now that his daughter has had a son, through an in vitro pregnancy, for some reason that Don can't figure out, she is keeping her distance from her parents. Don suspects that an honest discussion will drive his daughter further away, but he wants to take some action to ensure that he can develop a relationship with his grandson.

Although your issue may not identically resemble these scenarios, as you follow these stories throughout the book, you may recognize some familiar themes. Although specific issues differ, there are similarities in the general process that parents undergo when they make a commitment to provide appropriate and loving support to their adult offspring.

Under the avoid-meddling-at-all-costs model, some parents pretend problems don't exist, or quietly obsess about their children's problems and blame themselves. Parents who want to play a meaningful role in their children's lives instead choose the middle ground and attempt to figure out the appropriate action. The action may involve the child, or it may involve personal work only by the parents. Either way, effective parents operate from the point of view that they have a lot to offer their children no matter what their age.

Every situation is unique. There are no preordained formulas for success with a particular issue. But the process ahead will help you attain the objectivity and self-awareness necessary to take action that will help your child and enhance your relationship. The process requires love, honesty, commitment, and a pioneer spirit; and the possible benefits are immeasurable.

How Society Supports the Generation Gap

Parents who choose to work toward establishing a new tradition of closeness and connection are breaking new ground when they explore ways for their families to evolve into a healthy support system. Parents often find themselves feeling guilty about wanting to be "too involved" with their grown kids (even though there's no such thing as being too involved if parents are conscious of how they get involved). Understanding the societal component of these feelings may help relieve some of this unwarranted guilt while parents work to improve their relationship with their child. If you have qualms about your natural desire to work out a good relationship with your grown child, you probably are reacting to a social environment that scoffs at family ties. It's accepted as normal, even desirable, for parents and grown children to drift apart into superficial or hostile relationships.

We're surrounded by messages that support alienation between the generations. Product ads are full of disrespectful jokes about parents growing old and out-of-step with their grown kids but still insisting on giving advice. It's nothing new. There was a 1950s commercial where a pained-looking woman snapped, "Mother, please, I'd rather do it myself!"

Similarly, we get plenty of messages to support parental annoyance with grown kids. Television programs depict young adults returning home and exploiting their parents' resources. "She's only been visiting a few days and already she's run the car out of gas and emptied the fridge. Some things never change," a father says. Today there's a sarcastic new line: "Kids are like boomerangs, the farther your throw them, the faster they come back."

The popular notion is that separation from one's parents requires insulting repudiation. Society seems to view exasperation between the generations not as a sad commentary on the unhealthy state of the family, but rather as a sign of mature detachment. Perhaps it's because our culture places such a high value on independence that alienation from family seems to be a more acceptable alternative to the prospect of being enmeshed. But maybe we've gone too far.

Many self-help programs and therapists encourage people to "dump" their parents. Parents may be described as toxic or sick. Family attachments may be dismissed as dysfunctional or codepedendent. In this atmosphere, parents are thought to be doing their children a favor if they drop out of their kids' lives.

Parent-blaming is offered as a quick fix to personal problems. Parents have a huge burden placed on them. There are few realistic and popular images of good mothers and fathers in mainstream culture. By blaming their parents for their problems, grown kids can focus their attention on other people instead of engaging in the self-reflection necessary to confront difficulties head-on. They can oversimplify and complain about family instead of learning from the past and making positive changes.

Intuitively, most of us sense there's something wrong with this picture. It's absurd to believe that, in a few short years, people turn 180 degrees and change from bright-eyed children basking in the glow of parental attention into bristly adults warding off all attempts at parental influence. Even though that image seems false, it's very much part of an unspoken ritual of alienation that appears to have widespread acceptance.

Because of cultural influences and social pressures, parents may see alienation from their adult children as normal. Furthermore, for those parents who want to avoid the complexities of relationships, this view offers tacit permission to turn away when their kids are in pain or in trouble. For parents who are confused about their role with a troubled child, rejection can be the easy answer prescribed by someone outside the family.

The Price of Alienation

As a result of these social pressures on parents, some are walking away from, or being pushed away from, their adult children. Family is often relegated to a low rung on the priority ladder. It's easier to join the chase for success and material acquisitions than to do the more subtle, and often painful, work on relationships. Lifelong relationships don't happen without the occasional touching of raw and tender spots, which are primitive and intense. It can be simpler to put energy into more obvious and tangible activities.

But what happens when parents disappear from their adult children's lives? Even when they leave on request, they take with them the warm and protective psychic cloak that can come from feeling parental. Often, people need the sense of being loved more than they know, and don't miss it until it's gone.

One poignant example of alienation comes from the family of Senator George McGovern, who followed the advice of experts to cut off communication with his thirty-three-year-old daughter, Terri, an alcoholic and a drug addict. Her therapists believed it best for McGovern and his wife not to contact Terri, so she would take responsibility for her addiction. It was during this period of no contact that Terri died, after falling into the snow in a drunken stupor. In his laudable response to this tragedy, McGovern wrote a book, *Terri*, in which he entreats parents to stay close to their grown children, especially when they're in trouble. Senator McGovern's experience represents an extreme case, but it's a cautionary tale for people considering a hard-line approach that involves severing family ties.

Hope

You can choose connection and maintain or revive a relationship with a grown child that will enrich both of your lives. It's never too late to become a good parent. Even when a child's troubles stem in part from unmet childhood needs—when it really is the parents' "fault"—children can receive great benefit from parents who, even belatedly, learn how to demonstrate genuine love.

A great deal of family therapy involves examining issues from one's family of origin. At a time of crisis, the presence of loving parents—especially parents who have gone through an enriching process of personal growth—can have a healing effect on grown children.

There's a certain confidence enjoyed by people who are at ease with their parents, feel accepted by them, and feel safe to honestly express what's on their minds. It's as though they have a cushion in life. Although parents can't go back in time to provide the kind of unconditional love and support that are ideal when children are small, their approval and attention can be a source of comfort to their grown kids.

Leaders of the men's movement have been surprised to learn that, during "drumming" circles and other activities aimed at bringing men into harmony with one another, the participants discovered themselves wishing they could have a closer experience with their fathers. Some women have found in the goddess movement a way to tap into loving feminine energy they might have missed in their formative years.

Most people have an abiding connection with their parents that has great significance in their lives. Often, the bond is a quiet one, set apart from day-to-day life. But there's something warming about people who publicly share their relationship with their parents. That's why so many viewers love it when talk show host David Letterman invites his mother, popularly known as "Dave's Mom," to make one of her sweet cameo appearances on his late night show.

For many people who are alienated from their parents, contact may be infrequent but is so laden with meaning that even brief telephone discussions with parents can carry a heavy weight. In his autobiography, *Growing Up* (1983), the distinguished journalist and *Masterpiece Theater* commentator Russell Baker candidly describes the shift from his close boyhood relationship with his mother (his wife later called him a "mama's boy") to the strained relationship with his mother that prevailed during his adulthood. He matter-of-factly recounted the powerful push-pull connection with his mother, a connection that's almost taboo to discuss or even to acknowledge. The truth of parental relationships rarely becomes known to the individuals involved, much less articulately framed for everyone else to see. It's the ultimate exercise in objectivity. Baker's book won a Pulitzer Prize, in part because of his startling candor.

As a parent aware of your importance in your grown children's lives, you can help them find lenses that may help them see more clearly through the turbulent waters of family relationships. The biblical advice, "you will know the truth and the truth will make you free" (John 8:32), seems to apply to family systems, as well as to individual lives. Understanding familial relationships is a critical factor in your emotional health. Without such understanding, the people who surrounded you in childhood cease to be who they really are and turn into symbols. You can free yourself from the influence of these weighty symbols, and inspire your children to do the same, once you recognize the truth behind them.

Doctors James and Mary Framo, innovative family therapists, believe that the most effective form of therapy is to bring the whole family of origin into a room for a session that lasts several hours. When all are present in a safe place with a professional facilitator, adult children can communicate with the people who helped shape their lives. Expressing old pains and recognizing old patterns is liberating. Such elaborate therapy sessions may not be possible or practical for most people, but everyone needs to find ways to break free of old, suffocating roles in order to achieve more authentic relationships. Someone needs to bring some oxygen into the room, and it might as well be you.

Whether your goal is to strengthen your relationship with your grown child, release yourself from your child's dependency, or intervene in a crisis, you can decide to take a fresh approach. As a loving parent, you have tremendous power to breathe new life into family relationships. With this new model for lifelong parenting, you don't wait for your grown children to initiate such a connection; instead you create an atmosphere of openness that invites your children to make the connection when they're ready.

If you're facing a dangerous crisis involving the health or safety your grown child or grandchild, you may wish to skip ahead to chapters dealing with communication and intervention. In chapter 8, "Uninvited Intervention," there is a checklist to help you identify situations where you need to take immediate action. For most issues that come up with grown children, though, there's plenty of time for self-reflection before you decide how to reach out to your child. Generally, the issues are complex and require delicate handling.

What You Can Do

You can't go back and change the past, and you certainly can't change who your grown child is today. But you can make some personal changes that will allow you to express your love and commitment more effectively. Some actions you can take include the following:

- Help your grown child restore good faith in relationships

- Clear up old misunderstandings

- Find new ways to enjoy one another's company

- Make amends that can help heal your child's or your own emotional wounds

- Promote family traditions

- Exchange information about family history that will help your offspring develop objectivity

- Offer practical help to your child

- Provide support to help your children and grandchildren meet their goals

- Deepen your understanding of yourself, in a way that will enhance the quality of your life

Sometimes the heart's longing for closeness and the mind's hankering for understanding are at odds. It takes more than desire to move beyond habitual patterns of conversation and the fear of disclosure. It takes courage—especially if there has been a history of disappointment, alienation, or trouble—and it takes skill.

A Role Model for Personal Growth

You can identify what you symbolize in your child's life and use that knowledge to help them. You are the living history, the witness to your child's change and growth, the anchor to past and future hopes. Who else knows your child so intimately? Before your unique position in your grown child's life can be perceived as valuable, however, it's necessary to recognize the negative symbolism you may carry. Have your past critical words become an internal negative voice in your child's mind? Has your past rejection set your child on a course of seeking to have needs met inappropriately?

As you become more enlightened about the past, you can demonstrate the possibility for positive change in the future. If your children see the positive effects of self-awareness in your life, they will be more inclined to embark on a similar path of personal growth in their lives.

As psychologists come to understand more about the profound influence of family on the individual, it is becoming increasingly common for people to work on healing their relationships with their parents. Therapists frequently encourage clients to examine the influence of their parents, and literature often focuses on the powerful parent-child bond. There's a plethora of books available about how mothers and fathers affect their children, and what to do about those effects.

Many people—especially young adults busy with all the adjustment and survival issues typical of initiation into the worlds of work and marriage—may not have the time, energy, or inclination to devote themselves to such personal analysis. That's when caring parents can be of the most value. When parents begin doing their own emotional groundwork, they're starting the work for their children. Everything you learn about the constellation of factors that shaped you—and your parenting, your child, and the relationship between the two of you—can be of great value to future generations. As a parent willing to do the work toward achieving authentic relationships, by grasping the significance of your own family dynamics and sharing what you've learned, you will serve as both a model and a caring peer for your grown child.

CHAPTER 2

Voicing the Issues

In youth we learn; in age we understand.
—Marie Ebner-Eschenbach

No one can say of his house, "There is no trouble here."
—Asian proverb

There is a saying that one can judge the success of a society by the way it treats its less fortunate people. Similarly, one might judge a family by the way it handles its less pleasant issues. It's healthy to focus on positive interactions and devote energy toward creating pleasurable times together. Later in this book, you'll see some ideas for infusing new life into family occasions and making the most of one-on-one talks with grown children. Potentially joyful experiences can be thwarted, however, by unhappy undercurrents. Before genuine connection is possible, those undercurrents must at least be recognized.

Just as with other transitions in your life as a parent, you naturally have some questions about your role when certain milestones occur: When children go off to college or get their first apartment; when they are still living at home but reach chronological adulthood; when they give birth to children of their own; and/or when you retire and have more time for them.

Adjustments often occur naturally with agreements exchanged between you and your child that clarify practical questions. How often should you call the dorm? How does the family handle the grocery bill if you are all under one roof? How much will you be involved with your grandchildren? What do you want from your child now that you are getting older?

When It's Time to Regroup

It's inevitable, though, that you'll reach a point when your historic pattern of relating to one another isn't working. It can happen when your grown child is eighteen. It can happen when your child is fifty-eight. Suddenly, the issues are more complex than those that came up in the past. Something happens that brings a shift in the relationship. If you want to play a meaningful role in your grown child's life, you'll need to regroup.

The issues that create the need for this regrouping generally fall into one of three categories:

1. There's a strain in the relationship with your grown children or their families and you want to create more closeness.

2. You see that your child or grandchild needs help, but you don't know how to intervene.

3. Your grown child wants something from you, but you suspect it's unwise to give it.

It is a loving act to acknowledge troublesome issues that you face with a grown child. It may mean admitting that your child and your own parenting are not perfect. It also means that you care enough about healthy relationships to risk breaking habitual patterns, often perpetuated by denial, that are easier to continue.

Defining problems opens the door to real understanding, and it's brave to enter because there is no assurance of what lies inside. With the first turn of the knob, you can't expect to have the knowledge or objectivity necessary to see clearly all aspects of the situation. Some issues are merely worrisome. Others raise the specter of potential disaster. On the one hand, concerned parents are uncomfortable standing by quietly while their offspring's problems seem to escalate. On the other hand, they don't want to alienate their grown children. The question, How do I offer appropriate, loving support without going too far? is complex and not easily answered.

There are no simple answers, but the step-by-step process described in this book can help you develop the knowledge, self-confidence, and relationship skills necessary to provide loving support through the emotional highs and lows with your grown child. Unless you have a completely open relationship, however, it's best to do some emotional groundwork before approaching your child.

Framing the issue is the first step in preparing yourself to wisely handle your situation with your child. Being honest with yourself, having a discussion with your spouse, and/or talking with a friend are ways to get the subject out in the open. Problems immediately lose some of their bristles when they are removed from dark silence and examined in the light.

You can probably think of a specific experience that set off a small alarm in your mind signifying confusion or the potential for trouble in relation to a grown child. That's the starting point for a healthy analysis of the situation. As you think about whether any red flags have come up for you, consider these examples of how other parents came to recognize problems that required their attention. These people had a variety of experiences that brought to light a strain in relation to a grown child.

Alienation Issues

The first group of parents had problems communicating with their children and were feeling alienated from them.

Rosa

Rosa was having brunch at her home with her fiancé, a couple who had long been family friends, her three grown children, and their partners. At one point, she told a joke and everyone laughed, except her oldest daughter who said, "Mom, why don't you stop embarrassing yourself with those stupid jokes?" It was a typical remark for her daughter to make, and Rosa hardly noticed it, until she looked up from her eggs Benedict and saw that everyone around the table was sitting in embarrassed silence. At that moment, Rosa finally realized that her eldest daughter's habit of "dumping" on her was an inappropriate, backhanded way of expressing something serious.

Beth

Two weeks after her son and daughter-in-law canceled their trip to visit her for Thanksgiving, Beth made a seventy-mile trip to her son's town, pretending she was passing through on business, just to have lunch alone with him on a weekday. She had sensed some tension toward her from her daughter-in-law, and eleventh-hour cancellations were becoming a pattern. Beth wanted to find out what was going on. Yet when she was finally alone with her son, she didn't know what to say. It was the first awkward time in the twenty-five years of their close mother-son relationship.

Jake

"Oh c'mon Dad, don't tell me you're really going to leave all your friends. You'd go nuts in this town." That was the latest response from Jake's daughter to his earnest proposal to move closer to her

family. On past visits they had talked about how much fun it would be to live in the same town. Now he was finally retiring from the job that had previously torn him away from his family. He had assumed his daughter would enjoy having Grandpa and Grandma around for the kids, not to mention the time he and his daughter would have to get to know one another better. But after her latest hesitant response, he felt embarrassed about trying to have a frank discussion with her about the move.

Don

It was the second Christmas that Don's family was looking forward to spending with the newest grandson. Don offered to send airfare for his daughter, her partner, and their toddler to fly from California to Massachusetts; but they had refused the offer, saying they were getting together with friends instead. Don suggested some time in January or February, but they were all booked up. It seemed clear to Don that his daughter was avoiding getting together with her family, even though she and her partner had always come home for Christmas before their son was born. Don has worked hard to accept his daughter's lifestyle and lesbianism over the years, and he can't understand why she is keeping her distance now that she has her baby. Don feels that his grandson could clearly benefit from contact with a big, happy, traditional family.

Help Issues

In the second group, the parents felt that their adult children needed help, but they questioned whether they should step in—and, if so, how?

Sally

Sally went shopping for clothes with her twenty-two-year-old daughter one day and was surprised when Michelle suggested they go look at glassware and china. Michelle was thinking about getting married. Sally had met her daughter's new boyfriend a couple of times, but she couldn't believe it was a serious relationship. They were so different. He seemed to be as flaky and unambitious as she was bright and together. Why would she want to marry a man who works in a fast-food restaurant and seems to have no plans beyond that? Sally can't picture herself standing by silently as her daughter compromises her future.

Paula

Paula's middle daughter came for a visit with her toddler, leaving the older kids at home with their father. The poor woman was wiped out from her strenuous schedule, working full-time and raising three kids. Paula let her daughter sleep, played with her grandchild, and began remembering her own years as a working mom. When her daughter woke up, Paula tried to share some suggestions about how to manage the household, but her daughter just rolled her eyes and went back to sleep. Paula thought about writing down her ideas. Why should her daughter have to reinvent the wheel when Paula has the formulas that could save her daughter so much time?

Kathryn

Although Kathryn disliked her son-in-law, she was still determined to spend time with her daughter and young grandchildren, so every couple of months she would make the 500-mile drive to their home, sometimes alone and sometimes with her husband. Her daughter and son-in-law had an active social life, and Kathryn would offer to help when they were entertaining at their palatial home. On one weekend, during one of their frequent cocktail parties, she saw her son-in-law whisper something to a lovely young woman. The woman laughed, and then the two of them disappeared for a while from the crowd of about sixty chattering guests. Kathryn's daughter didn't seem to notice. Kathryn literally had to bite her tongue to avoid saying something. This wasn't the first time she had seen hints of her son-in-law's flirtations, but this time was the most flagrant.

Connie

Connie was reading a magazine article that listed the symptoms of depression, and found herself filling out the questionnaire with what she knew about her thirty-two-year-old son's recent slump. There were enough "yes" answers to make her question her earlier assessment that he was just "moping around" after his divorce. He might really need some help.

Anne

One day when Anne was visiting her daughter's home, her daughter told her five-year-old son three times to straighten his room. Only about ten minutes after he walked down the hall, her daughter was after the boy for not having accomplished enough. Later, when Anne went to say good-bye to her grandson, he whispered to her, "Could you teach me how to clean up my room sometime?" Anne

*could no longer ignore her daughter's lack of understanding of a
five-year old's capabilities.*

Michael

*Michael was in his grandson's room admiring a brand-new remote
controlled car. His grandson tossed it on the floor and said, "I'm bored
of it. My dad's going to get me a remote controlled boat!" Michael began
mentally calculating the cost of the toys in the room, and when he
reached $2,000, he felt sick. His visceral reaction made Michael realize
that his grandchildren's failure to appreciate their good fortune was
interfering with his enjoyment of them. He feels that somebody needs to
talk to these kids about the value of money.*

Mark

*Children typically get bumps and bruises during the normal
course of play, and Mark might not have thought twice about the ones
on his grandson if his son-in-law weren't such a harsh disciplinarian.
The boy looked at his father with fearful eyes and seemed withdrawn and
jumpy. But when Mark asked his daughter how everything was going,
she said their family life was great. Mark wasn't satisfied with her
answer and feels he needs to investigate the situation further.*

Inappropriate Help Issues

The next group of people faced issues in a third category. What should
parents do when grown kids ask for help that's questionable to give?

Tom

*Tom and his wife were home on a Sunday afternoon reading the
New York Times travel section. They were doing more than just
dreaming. Their house was on the market, and they were planning to
spend at least six months traveling. The phone rang. It was their
daughter. "I got accepted to law school!" she announced
enthusiastically. She had been working as a law clerk in a nearby city,
but now she wanted to quit her job. The law school was near the family
home, and she could devote herself full-time to school— if she could
move back in with her parents. Her mother was elated, and her first
response was "Anything we can do to help!" Tom, however, had a
painful vision of plans for the future dissolving if they supported their
daughter through three years of law school and did not sell the house.*

Lynn

When Lynn pulled into her driveway after work, the sight of her son's pickup truck made her heart sink. She dreaded walking into the house. What kind of mood would he be in? Would he be going to his Alcoholics Anonymous meeting, or was he drinking again? It had been a trying day, and Lynn just wanted to be alone. She'd tried everything possible to be a good parent to her son for forty-three years. Now he was depending on her again for room, board, and legal help.

Richard

Richard's four-year-old grandson ran outside and announced, "I want to do something, something fun!" The boy and his little sister had been sitting in front of the television for a couple of hours watching Saturday morning cartoons while Richard and his wife gardened. Richard felt annoyed. He didn't feel like entertaining the kids. He was enjoying the silent side-by-side digging in the dirt. The kids had spent a couple, or perhaps several, afternoons at his place during the past week; he'd lost track of how many days they'd come over. Usually he enjoyed throwing a ball with them or playing a board game. But at the moment, he just didn't want to interact. The prickly sensation of irritation surprised him. He adored these kids and often told others that he felt honored to spend time with them. But now he wished his son and daughter-in-law weren't so dependent on him for child care.

No Simple Answers

We have put these people's issues into three neat categories:

1. There are signs of alienation in the parent–adult child relationship.

2. An adult child needs help but doesn't necessarily want it.

3. The child wants help but the parent doesn't necessarily want to give it.

Unfortunately, there's no correspondingly simple way to categorize solutions. If life were simpler, the superficial advice of radio personalities or advice columnists would suffice. For example, one could say to Lynn: "You've done your job as a parent; if your son was stupid enough to drink and drive, that's his problem." Or to Kathryn, "Your daughter's husband is a no-good philanderer. Tell her to throw the bum out." Or to Beth and Jake, "Can't you take a hint? Get out of your kids' faces and get a life!"

But it's potentially harmful to a relationship to act on a knee-jerk reaction. Each situation is as unique as the individuals involved. For you to have a meaningful and positive influence, you'll have to go beyond the issue and examine the intricate personalities and relationships within your family.

For the people whose stories appear in this book, it took anywhere from weeks to years to examine and understand the complicated family systems that shaped their and their children's lives. Some sought counseling, others joined groups, and still others talked to spiritual leaders or did research by consulting with books, friends, or experts.

In all cases, their thinking became clearer and they felt enriched by the personal exploration, even if it did not lead to the result they expected. In many cases, the personal explorations preceded approaching their grown children about the troublesome issues. In other cases, parents began communicating with their children about pressing matters immediately. In still other cases, it turned out that once parents did their internal explorations, they found they didn't need to meddle in their children's lives, but instead began to establish a different, deeper relationship than the one they had had before.

This book will guide you through information and exercises that will deepen your understanding of yourself and your child so you can make your decisions with integrity. Ultimately, your action may end up looking quite different from what would work for someone else in a situation that seems similar to yours. Each person's process is different, but the steps can work for everyone. They include the following procedures:

- Stepping back to get a broader perspective on the problem, so you can be more effective

- Analyzing your relationship with your grown child, so you're in a better position to contribute insights

- Learning more about problematic parent-adult child patterns that you may be inadvertently perpetuating in your family

- Seeing how you and your offspring fit into the large picture of your family

- Fine-tuning your communication techniques

- Developing a strategy to cope with the challenges faced by you and your grown child

Telling Your Story

The best way to apply the information in this book to your own life is to use the writing spaces provided in this book to write your responses and observations. The first step is to describe the issue you are having with your grown child. As you proceed through this book, your assessment may change.

For now, do your best to find the words that will describe the issue accurately.

Exercise

Think back over recent conversations with your grown child. Was there a point where you felt ill at ease or confused about what to do?

Try to finish the following sentences, and continue writing as much as you can.

I am thinking about a time when

_____

_____

_____

_____

The issue with my grown child seems to be

_____

_____

_____

_____

This issue will become your window for looking at the constellation of factors that may be affecting your relationship with your grown child. How you handle this specific issue can be a blueprint for an effective demonstration of your love.

Surprising Perks

As you begin to look honestly at your relationship with your adult child, you will likely encounter unexpected perks. People who work to improve their relationships with their grown children have seen remarkable changes take place in their own lives.

Among these are the following:

- Developing strong connections with grandchildren

- Becoming more open not only with children but also with siblings and other members of your family

- Improving your ability to communicate with your spouse, family, friends, and co-workers

- Finding yourself infused with more energy

- Becoming more interested in outside activities, including hobbies and community work

Just by recognizing problems with your grown child, and beginning to work on them, you will experience some dramatic changes in your life, similar to the changes in the lives of those whose stories appear in this book.

Paula

At a women's retreat, Paula began coming to terms with her perfectionism and judgmental nature. She realized how hard she was on herself, which may have resulted in high expectations for her children. Of course, she'd like to see her grown kids do better with their parenting, scheduling, and money-management in their hectic lives; but she had to let go of her obsessive desire to "improve" them. She realized that in their childhood her criticisms had come across as messages of disapproval. As she began to let go of wanting to "fix" her kids' lives, she relaxed and shifted her awareness to herself, discovering how to have fun. She began to travel and made some positive shifts in her career. As her personal transformation progressed, her children became more receptive to hearing her ideas.

Lynn

As Lynn grappled with how to help her alcoholic son, she began attending meetings of Al-Anon and got involved in therapy. She explored her own history as a child who had been forced into early self-sufficiency and had become someone who put other people's needs first, taking responsibility for others but not getting her own needs met. As she began dealing with the issues from her own childhood, she began to make a more satisfying life for herself outside of her caretaker role. She found a boyfriend in Al-Anon and discovered it was okay to bring color into her own gray life, even while her son was struggling. As she began treating herself better, it was easier to feel love instead of resentment toward her son, and to learn the tools of adult parenting that proved valuable to his recovery.

Connie

To learn more about her son's depression, Connie saw a family counselor. There, she talked about a relationship with a sister who had tried to hide her depression. She then contacted her sister and had a frank discussion about their mother, who had been hospitalized for depression, which was something the people in the family had never discussed. Bringing the family's history of mental illness out into the open had the effect of improving Connie's marriage. She became more open to intimacy. Her husband was surprised to learn about her family history and the sad secrets she had kept. Looking at the "skeletons in the closet" created an opportunity to talk about feelings and fears within the marriage. Her husband began opening up as well. As a stronger couple, she and her husband began working together to figure out how to help their son with his issues.

Exercise

Take a moment to consider how issues with your grown child are affecting your life at present. Is your marriage influenced by concerns about your family? What about your work and social life—are they? Sometimes, the best thing you can do for the people you love is to take care of yourself.

In what ways would your life improve if you could feel assured that you were taking appropriate action, and thus could stop worrying about what to do about your grown child's problem? Would you like to:

- sleep better

- enjoy life more

- eat better

- talk about something else!

- fret less

- feel as though you're doing the "right thing"

- worry less about money

- feel more loving

- feel more relaxed

- lower your blood pressure

- stop having angry outbursts

- ease strain in your marriage and other relationships

- get out of the house more

- take a vacation

- take a class

Write down the answers that apply to you and include any other possibilities:

_____

_____

_____

_____

_____

Remember, often the best thing you can do for your family is to find contentment and satisfaction in your own life.

As you go through the information and exercises ahead, expect the unexpected! There's no end to the rewards possible when you bravely tackle your own issues, especially when you're doing so with the goal of strengthening your family.

As the great psychologist and philosopher Erich Fromm (1954) observed, mature love grows out of the knowledge that we receive in proportion to what we give. Love is more than a feeling, it is the decision to act in a loving way.

Each of us has the ability to move beyond surface relationships— leaving behind meaningless routines, controlling behavior, or cold distances of the past—and to choose instead actions that promote lively and nourishing interactions. It doesn't necessarily require more time than you spend together now, but it does take energy and creativity to transform the love you feel inside for your grown child into a palpable connection that will provide both of you with new strength and possibilities for growth.

CHAPTER 3

Gathering Perspectives

Philosophy is perfectly right in saying that life must be understood backward. But then one forgets the other clause—that it must be lived forward.

—Søren Kierkegaard, *Journals and Papers*

Like the sun which emits countless rays, compassion is the source of all inner growth and positive action.

—Tarthang Tulku, *Gesture of Balance*

The parent-child relationship can be a very intimate connection, full of promise for both of you. There are inevitable challenges over the years, but as a parent of a young child you understood your commitment and you had a clear role in your child's life. Now, perhaps at a time in your life when you least expected it, you are once again trying to cope with issues involving your child, but you may be wondering what approach you should take.

Before moving forward, it's wise to first become fully aware of where you stand now. It's essential to develop an objective view of yourself, your child, and the relationship the two of you share. There are techniques for controlling potentially harmful reactions that may interfere with your ability to act effectively.

Among the factors that stand in the way of objectivity are these: overly emotional responses, past memories invoked by the current situation, familial patterns of coping, and social pressures. These factors can be land mines unless you take the time to recognize how they are influencing the issue at hand. Regardless of your issue, you will approach it with more clarity and potential for success if you can defuse, or at least recognize, your own emotional hot spots. Your own reactions can weaken you and drain your energy if you do not have them in perspective.

If you don't have any immediate concerns, all the better. You can take the journey that unfolds in this book toward a greater self-awareness and a clearer view of your grown children. These steps are practical tools for keeping your extended family healthy and connected.

If, on the other hand, you're feeling an urgent need to do something immediately to solve a problem involving your child, you may balk at the seemingly cumbersome prospect of first doing some self-analysis. If that is the case, you may skip ahead to chapters 6–8, which offer guidance for communication, intervention, and limit setting; but it's wise to go through at least a short preparation phase before taking action.

You can establish a solid base from which to proceed if you:

- Identify your current emotions in the situation

- Examine your motivations for wanting to effect a change

- Understand family history that may, consciously or unconsciously, predetermine your attitude in the situation

- Silence a critical inner voice that may be blaming you for the problem at hand

- Define your view of how parents should relate to adult children

- Shed worries about "what people might think"

What Do Your Feelings Say?

Begin by recognizing your emotional reactions to any issue at hand. Go back to the last chapter and look at your written description of your specific issue. Read the words that you wrote and say them aloud to yourself. Pay attention to the feelings that surface as you consider what you are going through with your grown child. Are you perplexed? Sad? Angry? Frustrated? Anxious?

Here are some responses to these questions from other parents:

Beth
*"As my son slips further away from me, I find myself looking back
at his baby pictures and remembering the closeness we shared. I feel sad
as I remember our good times from long-ago. But when I see him now,
I'm kind of numb, unable to express my feelings."*

Recognizing a sense of grief over losing the past relationship with her son may help Beth move into an appropriate new phase.

Anne
"When I see my daughter nagging her son, I hurt with him. I'm sure she wouldn't do it if she understood more about child development. I love my grandson so much and feel deeply for him."

Realizing how much she empathizes with her grandson can be a signal to Anne that something from her past may be relevant to the current situation.

Jake
"It's confusing. My daughter always seemed to want more time with me. Now that I finally have the time, it seems like there's a wall between us."

Admitting he's confused can help Jake see he needs more information than he currently has about his relationship with his daughter.

Michael
"It rankles me when my grandkids demonstrate oblivion to their good fortune. I raised my own children to appreciate things. I didn't want other people to see them as ungrateful and irresponsible. My grandkids are exhibiting the very behavior I worked hard to train my kids to avoid."

Michael's annoyance over a perceived break with his value system may be interfering with his ability to look at underlying emotional issues.

Mark
"I'm furious and terrified that my son-in-law may be mistreating my grandson. I'm worried about my daughter, too. I sometimes have trouble sleeping because I can't stop thinking about it."

Mark's intense reaction carries a strong message that he needs to take action, but he needs to get a grip on himself so he doesn't lash out and make things worse.

Rosa

"I feel embarrassed and a little depressed over my daughter's disrespect toward me. I tell myself I should be happy at her success in life. But I feel as though I've failed."

Rosa's sense of shame may be interfering with her ability to respond appropriately to her daughter's poor treatment of her.

Kathryn

"I resent my son-in-law for flirting with other women and maybe even cheating on my daughter. Frankly, I'm also irritated with her. How could she be so blind and passive? I thought I raised her to be more savvy than that."

Kathryn's harsh judgment toward her daughter may be getting in the way of their relationship at a time when her daughter needs support.

Sally

"Shocked. That's the only description for the way I felt when my daughter talked about marrying the least suitable guy she's ever dated."

Realizing that she was caught completely off guard, Sally can become open to the possibility that she doesn't know her daughter as well as she thought she did.

Exercise

Identifying emotions is a starting point for unraveling a troublesome issue. Examine the feelings that come up when you think about something that's bothering you in relation to your grown child, and write them down. Try to finish these sentences:

Whenever I think about the problem with my child, I feel

_____

_____

_____

_____

My emotions may be telling me that

_____

_____

_____

_____

Recognizing feelings won't make them go away. Once you see how your actions are influenced by your emotions, however, you naturally will have more control over your behavior. Emotions tend to come from the unconscious, and as you become more and more aware of them, your conscious mind can exert more choice over what to do with them.

What Would People Think?

As a further step toward objectivity, pretend for a moment that some other parent and adult child are involved in your situation. Although we like to think that we place a higher value on what's objectively real than on our subjective perceptions, it can be instructive to view your situation as you think an outsider would see it. By asking the question, "What would I think if someone else had this problem and told me about it?" you can accomplish two things:

1. Recognize the kind of surface judgments we all make about families.

2. See past those judgments to the real business at hand.

Here are some ways that others have looked at their issues through "society's eyes":

Beth
"If you drift apart, you probably didn't have such a good relationship to begin with."

Jake
"If a friend of mine's kids didn't want him to move out near them, I'd say, 'Heck with 'em, you probably have better things to do anyway, buddy.'"

Anne

"People who have difficulty parenting need help, but not from their own parents—because their parents may have done a poor job with them."

Michael

"I'd think 'Your values must have been shallow if they weren't passed on to your grandchildren.'"

Mark

"If a friend had a grandchild who was being mistreated, I'd probably think there was something wrong with the whole family."

Rosa

"Anyone whose grown kid puts them down must have been a terrible mother."

Kathryn

"If a friend's daughter was being cheated on, I'd probably wonder why the mom had raised such a doormat. She should set her daughter straight, tactfully, of course."

Sally

"I'd wonder about a mother who was surprised at her daughter's choice in men. Maybe she didn't know her daughter very well."

When you say to yourself, "What would people think about my situation?" you may end up discovering it's the same thing *you* would think about *them* if they were in the same situation. Usually, your judgments about others reflect your judgments of yourself.

You can get some distance from the issue with your grown child, and insight into your own brand of self-criticism, by doing the following exercise:

Exercise

For a moment, pretend it's someone else who's dealing with your issue. Go back to your original statement of the problem in chapter 2, and read it aloud in a different tone than your usual voice. Picture someone else saying your words. Now write your thoughts by completing this sentence:

If someone I knew had a grown child in that situation, my judgment would probably be

_____

_____

_____

_____

Or, if it's easier for you to project your own judgments onto others, complete this sentence instead:

What would people think if they knew I had a grown child in this situation? They'd probably say

_____

_____

_____

_____

Reread your words. What can you learn about yourself?

Other parents learned a lot by stepping back from their problem and pretending it was someone else's. They got a glimpse of hidden judgments and emotions they did not know they were making or feeling.

Michael, Anne, Mark, and Rosa uncovered their deep belief that the problems of someone's offspring directly reflect on the parent's character or parenting ability. They'll have to get past self-blame before they can be effective.

Jake uncovered a resentment that could lead to him to reject his daughter. He's disapproving of adult children who do not welcome their parents into their lives. This realization may help him explore the possibilities for tactfully overcoming the barriers she's constructed.

Kathryn, by recognizing that she feels social pressure to help her daughter keep her son-in-law in line, can try to let go of feeling she has to fix the situation and instead focus on her relationship with her daughter.

Sally's "social judge" may be right—perhaps she doesn't know her daughter very well after all. Now she can try to change that.

Exercise

The exercise of viewing your family situation as an objective outsider is designed to help you attain some emotional distance, not to conform to some external idea of what's supposedly normal. As you read back your "If someone . . ." statement, what do you see about yourself? Write your impressions.

My external critic is telling me:

_____

_____

_____

_____

Realistic Expectations of Yourself

As you evaluate the role you have played in your child's development, be aware of the critical voice inside yourself. Although it's healthy to recognize past mistakes, you can become immobilized by harsh, repetitive self-criticism. Often, the nagging internal voice gives you damaging messages over and over, echoing the words from old family squabbles or rules imposed by society. Give yourself a break. You're working hard to be a good parent at a point when many people consider their parenting job finished. Many parents are unaware of the continuing effect they have on their children, but you're an exception. So, when your inner voice gives you a bad time, pretend there's a referee blowing a whistle that means "Stop." You don't deserve such harsh criticism.

Examine your own values so that you are less apt to be swayed by what other people might think. If you look for cues within instead of outside yourself, you may become more tolerant of yourself and others. You can get past superficial judgments and use what you know to deepen relationships for the benefit of everyone in your family. You're not entirely responsible for the choices your children have made in their lives. There are many other factors beyond one's parents that contribute to development, even though you have contributed, and still can contribute, a lot.

Nature versus Nurture

There are steps you can take to influence present and future environmental factors in order to be supportive of your grown child. It is important, however, to realize that there are biological factors that influence personality and behavior. Increasingly, research is proving that the way people respond to their environment has a strong genetic component. Some people are born with a genetic vulnerability to adverse circumstances. Biological factors heavily influence behavioral patterns, regardless of environment, according to a research project conducted by John Livesley, M.D., and reported in the *Journal of Personality* in 1966. Livesley's research was based on a study of 175 pairs of twins who clearly had inherited traits that influenced their behavior.

It's undeniable that environmental factors and the influence of other people also have a substantial effect on how the genetic predisposition plays itself out. Understanding the strong influence of biological factors can help you gain perspective, however.

Parents of Parents

As you examine your history of family relationships, one of your most powerful tools is your memory, not just your memories of yourself and your children, but also those about your own parents. Try to hold your parents in your mind as you go through the material in this book.

Exercise

Take a moment to ask yourself the following questions and then record your responses.

What do I most value about my parents?

_____

_____

_____

In what way can I be the same for my grown child?

_____

_____

_____

What do I wish I had received from my parents that I did not get?

_____

_____

_____

Am I providing this missing element for my child?

It cannot be overemphasized that the relationship with your own parents is integral to your relationship with your child. It is your blueprint, whether you are trying to follow it or to change it. The more you can consider your interactions with your parents as you work through the exercises in this book, the more likely it is that you will be able to clear your own path toward healthier relationships.

Your Family Tree

A family tree is a valuable asset for you and for future generations. It can be a rich source of information about your genetic inheritances, both positive and negative. Although parents and children are the direct carriers of family patterns, there's a lot to be learned from looking at other people who share your gene pool. When you look at your ancestors and descendants, individually and as they have interacted with one another, you may discover that even the distant past can shed light on situations now and in the future. Try moving beyond the picture of your adult child and yourself, and develop a perspective that takes in your entire family, including your parents, in-laws, grandparents, cousins, aunts, uncles, nephews, and nieces.

Were there success stories that might inspire your children to see new possibilities in their own lives? Has anyone in your family dealt with an issue similar to the one that has prompted your concern about your adult child? Think carefully about the family stories, and search for any situations that bear some particular resemblance to your own. You might call relatives to gather information you don't have readily available. It can be a great exercise for re-establishing connections in your extended family and for hearing some of the old family stories.

Draw your family tree in a separate notebook. Don't worry about neatness. If you like your rough sketch and decide to share it (it would be a great gift for family members), you can do that later. For now, choose any format that works to represent everyone in your family.

One common format is to place each generation on one line, representing males with boxes and females with circles. You might start with yourself and your partner (or ex-partner—whoever is the other parent of your children). Move down the tree with boxes and circles representing the children and grandchildren of you and your partner and your siblings. Move up the tree with boxes and circles that represent your parents, grandparents, and great grandparents.

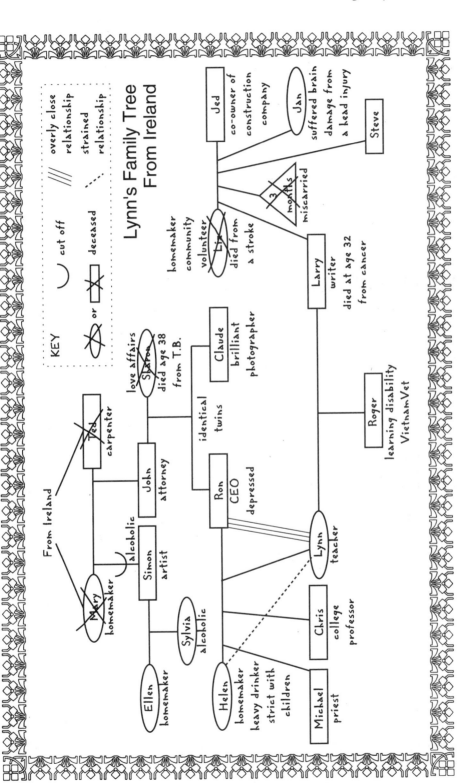

Include dates of birth and death, names and nicknames, occupations, accomplishments, personality types, memorable qualities, where they live, medical problems, tragedies and traumas, idiosyncrasies, religion, and any other pertinent information. Put an "X" through those who are deceased.

Consider not only the qualities of the individuals but also the quality of relationships between them. For people who became alienated, draw a slash through the line that connects them. For people whose relationships are particularly close, draw a double line. For people who seem overly dependent, draw a triple line between them. If you know some of the family secrets, such as abortion, mental illness, alcoholism or other addictions, or suicide, write them down. Look for patterns of events with recurring significance.

This family diagram may show how past events and relationships relate to current experiences of health and illness, success and failure, and some of the other ups and downs of life. You may see how certain activities are played out over and over, generation after generation. Pay particular notice to personality traits, rules, and strengths.

This exercise can be useful for seeing how issues currently involving your grown children may mirror a similar situation, or a pattern, that took place in the past within your family. Then you can examine how the situation in the past was handled, which may help you to decide on a course of action to pursue or avoid.

Here's how the construction of a family tree worked for others.

Beth
Beth took the opportunity to talk with her father and aunt who helped her draw a tree full of interesting characters who remained warmly connected with each other throughout their lives. The exercise started her thinking about her ex-husband's family, where there was a history of alienation between the generations. She began remembering how her husband seemed disinterested in his own mother, even though Beth would have welcomed a closer connection. It was hard for Beth to imagine, but maybe her son was drifting into a pattern similar to his father's, one generation earlier. To create a bridge between herself and her son, Beth began remembering and thinking about her own experiences as a young wife. Those memories helped her better understand her daughter-in-law. She also thought about her own family's successful traditions for staying connected. How did they do it? What could she learn from them?

Sally
Until she did her family tree, Sally had almost forgotten how many competent women had been among her ancestors. There were

teachers, nurses, a scientist, an architect, and a psychiatrist, back when it was rare for women to achieve in those professions. And many of these women had married men who had blue-collar jobs. They'd generally been happy and produced healthy, well-adjusted children. Although Sally had opted for the role of wife and homemaker, perhaps her daughter was following a family tradition. Sally began to think that perhaps an ambitious husband wasn't the most important thing in the world, especially if her daughter would continue to feel free to pursue a career of her own.

Richard

Richard was startled to discover how many people in his family had close relationships with one another. The revelation that his family had a long history of interdependence made him feel more secure in his relationships with his son and grandchildren. Strong ties, despite the ups and downs of family life, were part of his heritage.

Lynn

By doing her family tree, Lynn recalled a great-uncle who was an alcoholic. He was fine when he was "on the wagon," or so went the family lore. There weren't so many twelve-step programs back then, though there was Alcoholics Anonymous, but Uncle Simon didn't stick with it. During one "drying out" period, he married, had a child, and worked as a commercial artist. Apparently he was quite talented. What was it that turned him back to drinking? Realizing that there might be a genetic factor in her son's alcoholism helped Lynn to feel more sympathy for him.

Mark

Mark's family tree didn't reveal any history of violent behavior. In fact, kindness to others seemed to be a family value. But as he looked at the diagram of the tree and began thinking about family relationships, he recalled how rarely people had spoken about their feelings and personal matters. Avoiding problems was a tradition. No wonder he was having so much trouble dealing with a problem that was staring him right in the face. To get a broader perspective on the possibility of abuse in his daughter's life, Mark began thinking about his son-in-law's family. His daughter's husband had talked openly about disliking his own father. Recognizing the possibility that his son-in-law had had a difficult childhood softened Mark's anger. Maybe his son-in-law needed help.

A family tree is a visual tool that can help you understand how profound patterns are when they survive for generations. You may see positive traits that might be encouraged in your children and grandchildren. You may also see patterns of problems that can continue from generation to generation until they are recognized and handled.

Exercise

For the moment, try not to interpret the facts as you examine your extended family's history for situations similar to the one that your adult child is now experiencing. Try to remain as objective as you can.

Write down any and all situations from your family history that are similar in any way to the current problem. Finish this sentence:

Something in my family tree that reminds me of my grown child is

_____

_____

_____

Now, use your imagination to find any similarities between your adult child's current behavior and that of the person involved in the scene you just described. For the time being, set the differences aside and concentrate on the similarities. Finish these sentences

My adult child's strengths are similar to other family members in that

_____

_____

_____

My adult child's challenges reflect those of other family members in that

_____

_____

_____

Now, ask yourself what's the same—or different—about your response in the current situation, compared to the response of the parent of the relative with an issue similar to your child's. Then, finish these sentences:

From looking at family patterns, I can see that it would be consistent for me to respond to my adult child's problem by

_____

_____

_____

It would break tradition if I were to

_____

_____

_____

Why Do You Want to Help?

The next phase of this process is to identify your own motives for wanting to help your adult child. If your child or grandchild is in immediate danger, the answer is obvious: They need help, you love them, and there's no question that you must intervene. If this is the case, as it was for Mark, you're probably ready to take action now. If your child is in a life-threatening or dangerous situation, you'll want to skip ahead to chapter 8, "Uninvited Intervention," and come up with an immediate action plan. If you do this, also continue working through the other chapters. You'll need all the perspective, information, and insight you can get as you deal with the tough road ahead.

Most issues with grown children, though, do not involve emergencies. In most situations, the motivation for becoming involved is more subtle. Are you concerned primarily about your grown child? Or is your main worry how the problem reflects on you? Or are you upset about the feelings the situation arouses in you? Of course, your needs are important, but before you take any action, it's wise to separate your needs from the question of your adult child's well-being.

Before you begin to analyze your own motives, consider some of the reflections of others who are experiencing difficulties with their adult children.

Michael

Michael admits that his consternation over his grandkids'
behavior stems from his embarrassment in their presence. He wouldn't
want one of his friends to come over and see his grandkids acting so
badly. He also is concerned about their future, because he believes that
people do better in life if they're raised with manners and a sense of

values. He doesn't like the way his grandkids are preoccupied with acquiring things and are focused on clothes and toys instead of nature and community. Michael needs to sort out for himself to what extent he is acting from his own desire for decorum versus a true concern about the children's future. Is he reacting from the heart or from a desire to control?

Anne

Anne recognizes her deep empathy with her grandson and her feelings of responsibility for him, as though she were the only protector in his life. Before she can start to communicate with her daughter about the nagging of her grandson, she realizes she must examine why her feelings are so powerful.

Lynn

Lynn's motive is to find relief from pity for her son and the emotional drain that disappointment has caused. For years, she has searched for an antidote, a simple solution, and usually that has involved a "get-tough" stance that she cannot maintain. She has always ended up giving in to his needs and neglecting her own. But now she realizes she needs to confront her own feelings: Why can't she tolerate him getting mad at her?

Paula

Paula wants to help her daughter, who appears stressed and fatigued by the challenge of balancing her career, husband, children, and household responsibilities. Caught up in memories of her own struggles and sacrifices during her child-rearing years, Paula lost sight of her daughter's need to solve her own problems. She has a difficult time holding her tongue and overcoming her desire to control and judge. As she looks at the dark circles under her daughter's eyes, Paula feels so much sympathy that she wants to step in with advice before she is even asked. Paula needs to overcome her emotional response before she can provide respectful support for her daughter.

Rosa

Rosa's admission that she is depressed and ashamed might lead her to see that her motives for establishing a more mature relationship with her daughter are to relieve her own discomfort and to help her daughter become more self-aware.

Exercise

How about you? Are you clear about your motives for wanting to make a change in the relationship with your grown child? Write a brief statement, starting with:

The reason I want to take action in my grown child's life is

_____

_____

_____

_____

Once you have more clarification on your own motives, you can begin the process of separating your personal issues from your grown child's, thereby gaining a deeper perspective as you decide on a course of action. The goal is to gain at least a little distance from the situation, putting it in the context of a larger picture that involves your emotions, self-judgments, family patterns, personal needs, and any social pressures that may have influenced your past behavior.

Your Ideal

Another helpful exercise is to fantasize about the relationship you'd like to have with your grown child. A fully imagined fantasy can motivate you for the work ahead.

Here are some ways that others have envisioned their ideal parent-child relationship:

Lynn

*"I picture having a mature son who is responsible for himself
and a contributing member of society, drug- and alcohol-free. I imagine
myself relaxed and joking with him, introducing him to people and
feeling proud, and then going my separate way and not feeling
preoccupied, worried, and guilty about him. My whole body relaxes
just imagining this scenario."*

Rosa

*"In my ideal vision, I'm sharing a holiday with my daughter.
We're free to express our love toward each other and have forgiven each
other for the past. We're in the kitchen preparing dinner, laughing, and*

*there are few undercurrents of tension. She hugs me and gives me a kiss
and says, 'Thanks, mom.' It's really pretty simple."*

Tom

"I see my wife and me traveling around the world, and enjoying
visits with our grown children, who ideally are self-sufficient and happy.
Maybe we'd meet the kids abroad from time to time, as well as visit
them in their homes and have them over to the little condominium I
want to replace our big, old house."

Connie

"I imagine this: My family is all together and my son is in the
middle of the family circle, animated and involved. He's smiling, not in
a corner reading a magazine or taking a walk by himself, but
comfortably connected with the others."

Exercise

Take a moment to think about the vision you have of your relationship
with your grown child. Describe your vision:

_____

_____

_____

_____

_____

_____

Keep this vision in mind as your motivation for moving forward with
the process. The next chapter presents a refresher course on the stages of
adult development, to help you think about how natural transitions may be
affecting your family.

CHAPTER 4

The Cycle of Life

[N]o matter what our age, we are in our right place for where we are at that point in time, and we can freely develop our feelings of worth and take joy in this phase of our development.

—Virginia Satir, *The New Peoplemaking*

There are years that ask questions and years that answer.

—Zora Neale Hurston, *Their Eyes Were Watching God*

When a perplexing issue surfaces with a grown child, it's tempting to judge what's happening based upon past interactions. But you're likely to see the situation more clearly if you recognize that both of you are constantly changing. Understanding the nature of that change will enrich you as an individual and strengthen the connection between you and your child.

The landscape of the parent-child relationship is filled with hidden land mines that can explode at any time, not always because of something you do "wrong" but because of the potential for misinterpretation. For example, one woman called her son at college to ask him a practical question about how to run a piece of equipment. She began the conversation with a casual "How are you?" and in return got a huffy response, "Mom, I wish you wouldn't freak out." It turned out he'd been ill and assumed she called because she was worried about him.

When seeking to play a meaningful role in the life of your grown child, it's helpful to keep in mind where everyone is "at" in terms of personal development. Later in the book, we'll explore the particular aspects of your own family dynamics, including how your parenting affected your child's development and what you can do with that knowledge.

As a parent, it's a challenge to become a peer. Your relationship may evolve into friendship, but mostly likely it will always include some expectations and assumptions based on your earlier parent-child relationship. Opportunities for meaningful communication improve when family members recognize that individuals continue to develop and change over the years. Just as children go through predictable stages in their younger years, the adult years also follow a typical pattern. Understanding the adult stages of life can benefit everyone.

Adult Stages

Briefly reviewing theories of human development may offer you some new insights into psychological influences affecting you and your child and shed some light on your current issues. At various phases of life, people necessarily undergo certain challenges that alter their behavior and change the way they relate to their parents. Your adult child's present behavior may be due, in part, to a stage of growth that is quite normal, even though the manifestation may be troubling. If you can understand some of the "why's" of the problem, you will find yourself in a better position to uncover the "how's" of a solution.

You may be operating under a false assumption that just because you and your child are both adults you share similar outlooks, desires, and needs. That was once the common wisdom. Until the early twentieth century, it was thought that growth and development were essentially finished at the end of adolescence. But research by psychologist Carl Jung (1957) shed new light on the complexities of the life cycle.

Jung observed that people spend the first forty years of their lives forming a strong relationship with the outer world and the second forty on inner growth. That people continue evolving throughout their lives is now an accepted fact. Each season of life brings with it an opening for certain types of personal growth. Several research psychologists have made systematic studies about adult development that give us a framework for understanding what's happening in our individual lives.

Individuals go through distinct phases in their lives. Research psychologist Charlotte Buhler was among the first to theorize that adult lives are divided into several distinct periods. Hers was the first major study, and paved the way for Erik Erikson (1950), Bernice Neugarten (1968), Roger L. Gould (1972), and Gail Sheehey (1977) to develop more in-depth research and theories on the stages and overall pattern, or design, of human life.

They all perceived that individuals move between periods of transition and periods of stability, generally for about twenty years each.

In 1972, Gould, a medical doctor at University of California at Los Angeles, published the results of a study of 524 men and women he had interviewed over a period of years. He noted that as they aged they became more self-accepting. Among his findings:

- The age group from sixteen to eighteen-years old is characterized by the motto "We have to get away from our parents." While proclaiming autonomy, people of this age group are likely to have a precarious hold on independence.

- The twenty-something years are marked by great confidence and optimism and the continuation of the desire to separate from their parents. People in this age group re-create the safety of the family through the formation of strong peer groups.

- By the end of their twenties, most people feel quite established and engage in the self-reliant work of adult life.

- People in their thirties are more self-reflective, with concerns about what they are doing and why. Life is seen as much more difficult and painful than it appeared in their twenties. This is a time when they no longer need to prove themselves to their parents or to stress their differences. They feel more free to acknowledge and accept parts of themselves as being like their family of origin.

- The forties bring an awareness that time is finite, youth is slipping away, and death is inevitable. Most of Gould's subjects felt they were in their prime and recognized they were at a mid-point in life. There was a realization that there was little time left to shape the behavior of their children.

- People in their fifties find an eagerness to have more human experiences rather than searching for material things, glamour, and power. People in this phase feel more fully in charge of their lives, particularly toward the end of the stage. For some, the advancing of age spurs them on to further accomplishments and pleasures in the time left to live. Relationships with their own parents usually mellow and there tends to be some resolution of tensions.

- Priorities continue to shift gradually when people are in their sixties. Marriage satisfaction often climbs. With their children grown and gone there is an opportunity to experience a life of fewer responsibilities.

- The seventies bring a renewed questioning about the meaningfulness of life and further review of one's contributions.

People can achieve a dramatic, positive turnabout later in life when they have time to develop their inward lives. Many men, for example, who in their younger years were completely distracted by the world of work and had little time to understand the psychological or spiritual needs of those around them, develop their nurturing, vulnerable aspects and discover the value of close connections with others later in life. They talk about feeling grateful that they still have time in their lives to explore the new worlds of personal relationships. Perhaps it was a man in this stage of life who came up with the well-known saying: "No one ever said on their deathbed they wish they'd spent more time on business."

Similarly, women who were once full-time homemakers and mothers—some of whom were so involved in their role as caretaker that they temporarily lost their own identities—find that after their children are grown they are ready to explore the world. Many former "homebodies" transform into career-focused women whose ambitions spring from a desire to meet their personal needs. Of course, the opportunities for change are not gender-specific. Both men and women are likely in later life to find new possibilities and passions during this time of renewed creativity.

When Parental Stages Clash with Children's

When looking at your particular family situation, it can be instructive to keep in mind where each person falls within the stages of development. Certain combinations of developmental stages can make for more conflict and tension than others, especially if two or three people are going through major transition periods at the same time.

For example, if you are going through a midlife transition (age forty to forty-five) while your young adult children are making the change from adolescence to early adulthood this could make for a volatile time. While they're wrapped up with the tasks of maintaining autonomy and sorting out the pressing demands of relationships with a mate and an employer, you're juggling your priorities and possibly looking for a shift in your career, marriage, and fundamental requirements. Both you and your children are at a stage that offers opportunities for new growth, but at the same time, these stages may create anxiety about the future. Both you and your children will be challenged to outgrow immaturities and illusions of youth and build fuller, more balanced lives.

Here are some ways that people have seen challenges with their grown children in the context of their phases of life.

Tom
Now in his late fifties, Tom realizes he will soon be completing the phase of his life that involved full-time work. He is ready to embark on a

new phase that will mean finally getting to accomplish goals that he has had to put off during his child-rearing years. His daughter's desire to return home threatens his sense of freedom and optimism about what he considers a "last chance" to finish some personal projects. At the same time, he recognizes that his daughter, at twenty-four, should be developing autonomy. To Tom, her desire to return home seems to reflect a failure for both of them. Before he makes any decisions about his daughter, he needs to define just what it is he wants to do at this point in his life, so that he can be more clearheaded when dealing with her.

Rosa

Rosa has heard the term "midlife crisis" over and over but she never thought of it applying to her. And yet here she is in her late forties, evaluating her values and experiencing upset over the relationship with her daughter. Her daughter's put-downs bring up feelings of inadequacy that Rosa now realizes have plagued her for several years.

Her goal is to mend the rift, but she sees the need to first gain a clearer understanding of her own feelings in this time of transition. In a way, this has become a time of "comeuppance" for Rosa, and her daughter appears to be the accuser. At the same time, it's obvious that her daughter is thriving in her own life, perhaps drawing a line in the sand to define her own autonomy. Rosa and her daughter are both undergoing major life transitions. Is there a way Rosa can see that her daughter's behavior springs from her need for distance, which coincides with Rosa's own need to take some time for solitude and to evaluate her life?

Jake

Jake is enjoying a time of unprecedented openness. For most of his life, he kept his feelings inside, not wanting to be viewed as weak or unmasculine. Now, he has entered a stage of development when he no longer wants to deny his feelings. He acknowledges a sense of loneliness and the desire for a deeper connection with his family.

Now that he is retiring, he has the luxury of focusing on what's most valuable to him and making the choice to spend his time with family. In his late sixties, he sees his daughter and grandkids as a priority, but his daughter isn't open to his discussions about moving closer to her.

It helps him to realize that, in her midthirties, his daughter is caught up in the busiest time of her life. It takes all of her energy to work at her part-time job and maintain her involvement in her children's lives. She might not have the extra ounce of energy necessary to

consider her father's need for some clarification about his possible move.
        Jake realizes he can't assume that his daughter's unresponsiveness
means rejection. It's up to him to define what kind of role he'd like to
play in her life and initiate a discussion, keeping in mind that his
daughter may not be in a position to meet his needs and that he should
be creative in considering how he might meet some of hers—by being an
involved, accessible grandfather.

Growth Through Self-Reflection

At the same time that you are getting in touch with new aspects of your life, your grown children are absorbed in their own lives. But at some point they'll need to embark on the necessary but often painful process of reflecting upon how family patterns have affected them.

Ideally, people begin examining the influence of family on their lives while they are still in their twenties, but this may not occur until they have reached their thirties or forties. While people begin this process at different stages in their lives, the sooner it happens, the better, as this provides them with greater self-awareness to enhance their life experiences.

Drs. Gay Hendricks and Kathlyn Hendricks (1990), in their book, *Conscious Loving: The Journey to Co-Commitment,* argue that transcending childhood conditioning is one of the most important steps in adult life and that people cannot attain peace and happiness until they do so. The Hendrickses believe that many people go to elaborate measures to avoid dealing with troublesome issues from childhood. But those who lose themselves in work, addictions, or other diversions are only making the inevitable more difficult. They write: "These issues come politely knocking at our door in our twenties, then rap louder in our thirties. If you delay looking at your programming until your forties, you are likely to get the message delivered with sledgehammer blows."

Some adults get stuck in a particular phase of development because of an early trauma. To move forward, they need to go back and work through their feelings about what occurred. There are others who behave appropriately for their stage in life until times of high stress, when they quickly regress to an earlier stage. These people need to find tools for coping with stress.

We can help our grown children make appropriate movement along the developmental continuum by doing so ourselves. People who undergo self-reflection with the goal of personal growth become role models for their grown children. It's not something you can come out and advise your children to do, but by taking the time to develop an objective view about your own life stages, you'll be subtly encouraging them to do the same.

The Transition from Adolescence to Adulthood

Researchers of the life cycle found that each period of development brings both painful and gratifying aspects. How people respond depends not just on the individuals but also on family traditions and the larger culture. Cultures vary in their support of and respect for people at different stages of development. The social context can have a profound effect on relationships.

It's difficult to come into adulthood in American society in part because the transition phase—adolescence—is so often a disrespected life stage. There seems to be an inherent, pervasive mistrust of people in their teenage years. There's an expectation of rebellion that can become a self-fulfilling prophesy.

Even though we may have shocked our own parents with the fashions of our adolescent years—whether that was bobbed or long, stringy hair, tight jeans or hip-hugging bell bottoms—we still may be disapproving of teens who sport nose rings, pink hair, or jeans worn so low that the pockets are at the knees. Think about what it means to go straight from the status of a social "outsider" as an adolescent in our culture to the status of an adult who is suddenly expected to become a productive member of society.

In many cultures, the transition from childhood to young adulthood is marked by a welcoming ritual that acknowledges the change as positive. Anthropologist Colin M. Turnbull (1961), in his study of South African pygmies, *The Forest People*, describes a moving ritual for young women.

> They sang songs whose words had no particular significance, but which in themselves were of the greatest significance, being songs sung only by adult women. That was why so many of the mothers and grandmothers had assembled, to welcome their daughters into their midst again, no longer as children, but as friends and partners in adult life. Some of the women looked sad, for they knew that this meant that the girls would soon get married, and then they would almost certainly leave to join their husbands in other camps.

In our society, some families use religious rituals such as the Catholic confirmation sacrament or the Jewish Bar Mitzvah or Bat Mitzvah coming-of-age ceremony as a way to acknowledge the transition to adulthood. But such conscious welcoming of young people into the adult world is the exception rather than the norm. Though we can't help being influenced by how our culture treats different age groups, we can choose within our own families to develop traditions and rituals that celebrate the different stages.

Even without a religious or cultural model, more and more families are finding their own way to mark adolescence as an exciting passage by celebrating the child's growing autonomy with public rituals, while developing tolerance for the inevitable badges of independence that take the form of seemingly bizarre fashions and activities. In return, parents get the trust and the benefits of an ongoing connection, which endures as the child ventures farther and farther from home. Realizing that our society neglects the adolescent passage can help us empathize with people who embark on adulthood without the confidence or preparation necessary to handle adult responsibilities.

Recalling Your Child's Transition to Adulthood

If you're like most parents, you probably look back at your child's entry into adulthood—those difficult adolescent years—with a mixture of regret and amusement. It's important to examine this period that immediately preceded your child's ascension into adulthood, and the part you played. You might uncover some leftover feelings of abandonment or resentment—on your part or your child's—that still affect both of you.

We all have some warm memories, to be cherished and passed along, about the magical moments that signify a child's movement into adulthood. Usually, though, we also have an equal number of regrets. Many people look back and wish they had reacted differently when they were caught up in the inevitable power struggles while they were in their teens. The episodes of friction can end up dominating our memories, so that later we're more inclined to recall the bitter times than the sweet celebrations.

Some parents agonize over their child's transition into adulthood. Parents may be sick with worry when their kid takes off for the big city or perplexed over their kid's decision to experiment with a different religion. Others may experience devastation when their grown child hooks up with "losers," experiments with drugs, or comes up with a lifestyle that seems purposefully designed to run counter to their family's values. It's tempting to blame a child if they choose a rocky road toward adulthood that causes pain for them and their parents. Parents can carry resentment for years, especially if their kid's decisions directly affect their own lives in a negative way. Out-of-control kids can cost parents friends, money, time, and energy.

Exercise

To ensure that you are not carrying a grudge about your child's adolescent behavior, write on the lines provided below the things your child did that irritated you or perhaps even felt like a betrayal:

_____

_____

_____

_____

Parents Get Separation Anxiety, Too

Looking back, many parents see that they were too self-involved to offer the love and compassion their teenagers needed to make the successful transition to adulthood. As an older parent, you may come to an awareness that you unwittingly played a part in pushing your child down a rocky road toward adulthood. You may desperately wish to be able to go back and give your kid a better preparation for the tough world. While you can't do that, you can reach a deeper understanding of the complexity of the life stage that immediately precedes adulthood.

Part of the struggle for control between young adults and parents is that the parents are suffering from their own anxiety about separation. They see their children yearning for freedom and beginning to find their way through life on their own terms. They must let their child go out into the dangerous world. There are kids who don't make it, kids who commit suicide, overdose on drugs, or are murdered. These harsh realities heighten parental anxiety. The fear is real. But children can't be protected forever.

Another separation issue is parents letting go of ambitions for their children. In some cases, parents need to let go of their illusions about who they want their kids to be and accept who they are. Letting go is painful. There's no way to make it easy. It usually helps parents to know that there are steps they can take to stay close and be available if their child needs them.

Sally

Sally's daughter was the classic twenty-something, optimistic and very involved in her peer group, while Sally herself was a classic change-of-life fifty-year old. While Sally was dealing with a difficult menopause, experiencing insomnia, weight gain, aches, and mood swings, her daughter was just beginning to think about marriage. Worrying about her daughter's choice of mates was a way for Sally to hang on to her parenting role. Although Sally always had considered herself a thoroughly modern woman, she was actually having trouble letting go of her daughter. Once Sally was able to see that she was experiencing some separation anxiety, she was in a better position to look clearly at how she wanted to live the next phase of her life—and to focus less on exerting control over her daughter's choices.

As you proceed with the personal work necessary to become an effective supporter of your grown child, it will be helpful to take a look back at the way you dealt with your child's transition to adulthood. Later on in the process, when you're ready to communicate, you can share these memories to help increase your children's awareness of the factors that shaped who they are today. Your honesty has the potential to build bridges between you and your child that may have been long in disrepair.

Exercise

Look back at your grown child's adolescence. Write about how well your child was prepared for adulthood, and what might have made the transition easier.

My child faced these challenges in adolescence:

_____

_____

_____

_____

My child's movement into the adult world might have been more comfortable if

_____

_____

_____

_____

Moving into the Older Generation

It's a natural rite of passage for parents of young adult children to get a flickering of awareness that what lies ahead for them, albeit a ways down the road, is their own status as a senior—or, as humor columnist Dave Barry puts it—their "elderlyhood." One of the more startling aspects of aging is the subtle process of "trading places" that occurs as you and your children grow older. At some point, you'll begin losing physical strength and earning power, and, while you can plan ahead for most eventualities, probably some part of you hopes your child will be available to give you care and nurturing in your old age. If your grown kids are having difficulty in their lives, there may be a voice in your mind whispering, "What happens when I can't take care of them anymore—or if I need them to take care of me?"

You can't wait for your children to bring up this topic of concern. Aging is a taboo subject in many families, reflecting our youth-oriented society's general lack of respect for the elderly. Unlike other cultures that revere their elders, we lack traditions for treasuring the wisdom and vision of older people. But there's a lot you can do within your own family.

You can continue exploring ways to contribute to the lives of your children and continue to develop your own interests. People who embrace the later phases of life will find ways to share their wisdom—with family and the larger community—as volunteers, active grandparents, recorders of history, coaches, artists, and teachers of one kind or another.

You can recognize that it's not only for your emotional health but also for the mental health of your child that you maintain a sense of self-respect as the years go by. The love from one's parents is a critical factor in well-being, regardless of age. From birth until the parents' deaths—and sometimes, symbolically, beyond the parents' deaths—people seek to love and be loved by, to respect and be respected by, their parents.

You can take a leadership role in opening lines of communication about how you see your future. Most children are relieved when parents talk about such difficult matters. Much future grief can be saved by a proactive discussion about where you want to live if you become immobile, what kind of medical treatment you want if you become so ill you can't communicate, how your financial resources should be handled, and even what kind of memorial you want for yourself. Many families find these discussions easier with the help of estate planners or members of the clergy. Other families, who do not have a history of open communication, can begin handling these issues by writing letters.

As you become more comfortable dealing with difficult topics, intergenerational relationships will grow stronger. In an atmosphere where people can be frank with one another, there's room for an open exchange of ideas. You can define the offerings you have for your family at this phase of your life. For some people, it takes a crisis, or a threat of impending stagnation, to recognize it's time to create a new place for themselves in the family.

Jake

Jake retired against his will. He had to leave his company because of a downsizing. It was a shock to him because of his loyalty to the company for thirty years. This crisis may have contributed to his increased sense of vulnerability. He has a strong desire to pass along what he knows to future generations, and this is manifested in his desire to move closer to his daughter and grandchildren. He is beginning to envision himself playing with model trains with his grandkids. His values are changing. But as much as he wishes to express tenderness, his vulnerability comes across to his daughter as neediness. His daughter suspects he is now turning to her for support, and she doesn't yet know, based on the past, about what he can offer to her. If Jake can realize the significance of his current stage of life and become more articulate about his desire to redefine his role in his family, it may relieve his daughter's fears that she will be expected to cater to his needs—and perhaps make it easier for her to accept what he has to give.

A Different View of Aging

In our society—where fighting signs of age is a national obsession and a multibillion-dollar industry—we may have to work diligently to carve out a meaningful role for ourselves as we age.

In some cultures, it is understood that the elders enjoy a respected place in the family, and the younger people look to them for approval and guidance. It can be startling—and heartwarming—to glimpse the positive light in which elders in some societies bask. Eileen Clegg's mother, Iris Ridgway, tells a delightful story about how she discovered the East/West difference in the perception of aging. She teaches English as a Second Language at a junior high school. One day, Iris ran into a Laotian boy who was a former student of hers. Now, a junior in high school, he had changed dramatically since she had last seen him in the eighth grade. "My goodness, you certainly look older!" Iris exclaimed. He smiled and returned the compliment, "Thank you, and so do you!"

In the eyes of this young Southeast Asian man, it was a high compliment to tell a woman in her sixties that she was showing her age. In his culture, older people are cherished and respected. Quite a contrast compared to American culture, where retirement and old age often open the door to the realm of isolation. No longer seen as an asset, many seniors suffer from their societal loss of role and status.

By working to play a meaningful part in your grown child's life, you are leading the way toward redefining the place of elders in your family. Many families are returning to the view that the older generation is a collective asset. Grandparents are encouraged to spend time with their grandchildren, with the idea that both can benefit from the exchange of wisdom and affection. The special kind of love that grandparents can offer to young ones is appreciated at a time when parents are busy with the demands of work and building a life together.

Iris Ridgway has taken to calling her family a "tribe," because even though relatives live at some distance from one another, there's a shared family value that the kids "belong" to everyone. Aunts and uncles compete for visits from the kids during summer vacations and regularly exchange phone calls to help with homework and to hear what's happening. Iris pays attention to issues that are affecting her children and grandchildren and tries to find ways to share her ideas "without meddling," using self-analysis and communication. She inspired some of the techniques that are presented in this book. Her ideas are usually helpful and well-expressed, but not always. Either way, her children and grandchildren trust her love and motives, so the lines of communication remain open.

Maintaining a Respected Place in the Family

Feeling loved by one's parents is a great asset to an individual's emotional health, regardless of age. Although intellectually aware of their potential for giving to the younger generation, many older people get messages from society that make them feel diminished or disposable as they age.

Beth

Beth derived a lot of her confidence from her success in "a man's world" as an engineer designing airplanes. When she was diagnosed with breast cancer, she lost work time and suffered from the stigma of being ill. Suddenly she found herself being treated differently, without the respect that her leadership position had provided for her in her profession of twenty years. It was hard enough for her to muster up the emotional courage to reach out to her son and daughter-in-law, but her loss of status and her energy-draining health problems made her feel even more insignificant as a person. However, her love for her son, and her deep awareness of her importance to him, gave her strength to pursue ways to bridge the growing distance between them.

Don

Don had always enjoyed his role as patriarch of the family, presiding over traditional gatherings where he exuded charm and shared colorful stories. In the past, he had had few real day-to-day child-rearing duties with his own children. Now he could see, with regret, that he had been stern and aloof with his daughter. He had expectations of how a grandfather should be involved in a grandson's life, but the alienation from his daughter could prevent Don from developing a close relationship with his grandson. He felt frustrated that his past mistakes were hindering his hopes for the future and was sad that he didn't have a better relationship with his daughter.

Life challenges can impinge on the parent–adult child relationship by subtly eroding your sense of belonging and importance both in the world and in your family. But there are few circumstances that can diminish the leadership that parents can bring to the family. If you begin to doubt for a moment how important you are to your children, stop again and remember your feelings toward your own parents. What did their love mean to you? In what ways did they enrich your life as an adult? In what ways did you wish for them to be involved in your life?

Exercise

Take a moment once again to write some reflections about your parents. Try finishing this sentence:

My parents' love meant that

_____

_____

_____

If we can truly comprehend the importance of parental love, we will be motivated to find ways to become a healing and loving influence within our families. The challenge is to do so in appropriate ways. It helps to take the long-term view, taking into consideration the respective life stages of the family members involved. Like the seasons of the year, each life stage is marked by its own tasks and character, leading to an outcome that reflects a full, natural cycle.

Exercise

Once you begin to separate the issues specific to your phase of life from those specific to your child, you'll likely find it easier to communicate. As an exercise, make a list based on the phrase below. Obviously you won't have all the answers, but write down any words or phrases that come to mind. Your intuitive first thoughts will tell you a lot. Write as quickly as you can without editing or questioning. Then review the list.

At my phase of life, my challenge is to

_____

_____

_____

Exercise

Now ask yourself: At this stage in my life, what do I need to do for myself?

_____

_____

_____

Then, finish this sentence: At my child's phase of life, the challenge is to

_____

_____

_____

The remainder of the book will be devoted to finding an answer to the question, "Given our respective stages in life, what can I do to be a loving and supportive parent, while fostering my own and my child's best development?"

Keep this question in mind as you move on to chapter 5, which is devoted to laying the groundwork by reviewing—and perhaps renewing—your commitment to your child.

CHAPTER 5

Evaluating the Relationship with Your Child

In the Chinese language, the word "crisis" is written with two characters: One means "danger," the other means "opportunity."

There are no perfect parents! What's important is that you try to keep moving in that direction and to be honest about where you are. Admit it, and then learn together. Your children's trust in you will increase rather than decrease.

—Virginia Satir, *The New Peoplemaking*

You're well on your way to becoming a more supportive parent simply by having the desire to gain new knowledge and skills. Your current effort to improve the relationship with your grown child probably is motivated by feelings of love and a desire for trust. But before taking action, you first may need to look past bouts of alienation or miscommunication. To establish or re-establish a loving connection with your grown child, you might take an honest look at the factors that may have eroded your bond in the past. Begin with a memory of the love you felt for your newborn.

Recalling the Magic of the Newborn

Let yourself go back to the weeks and months after your child was born. If you bonded with your child, the miracle of this new person washed over you and left you drenched with feelings of love and protectiveness and the resolve to give this lovely, helpless being as much care and affection as possible.

Indulge yourself with your memories. Look at their baby pictures. Recall the books you read to your children out loud. Remember the hopes you had for them and the possibilities you envisioned for your parent-child relationship. Back then, you intuitively knew that your love and care would have an incredible influence on the kind of people your children would become. You were in awe of the new life.

Now that your child is grown, your influence may seem nil. You have grown, too, and you may look back and see ways that you could have been a better parent. All parents make mistakes, and conscientious parents often suffer if they believe that their adult children's problems result from something that was lacking in their upbringing.

Rediscovering the Magic

The good news is that it's never too late to help heal some of your child's—and your own—pain that may stem from long-ago difficulties. As you proceed through this chapter, remember that there are no perfect parents. There are those who try and those who do not. Because you are reading this book, it is clear that you are one of those who is trying. Remember to give yourself credit for your efforts.

It can be valuable to both parents and children take a look back at difficult past experiences. Your child might still be left with some unresolved childhood hurts or fears, and they may be contributing to today's difficulties. You can help, but only if you're brave enough to get through the guilt—or denial—that immobilizes many parents. Call upon the love you have for your child to inspire you to be honest with yourself about past factors that may figure in today's issues.

If you are willing to acknowledge your own past parenting flaws to yourself—and eventually admit them to your child—you can help free them from old patterns. It is never too late to help your child reach closure on past issues. Recognizing the nature of one's childhood difficulties is necessary for maturity and healthy relationships.

Obviously, you are not solely responsible for the kind of adult your child grew up to be. You can't take full credit for the successes nor full blame for the failures. But if you can become honest and clear about your past parenting practices, you will be in a better position to provide the love and support that are needed now.

Try to set aside any self-recriminations and move into a more objective mode. This way, you can accurately assess the information about the past so that you can embark on a healthy plan for sharing your wisdom with your child. Everyone will be healthier for it.

Becoming Aware of Past Parenting Practices

Children need unconditional love to thrive. At the same time, even for the best of parents, unconditional love can be difficult to maintain or to express. Therein lies the root of most parent-child difficulties. The inevitable fall from perfect love can lead to disillusionment. When love is withheld—or given with unrealistic demands for equal or greater love in return—children may sustain emotional scars.

It's useless to get stuck in self-blaming, but it's possible to recognize your mistakes so you can help your children recognize the factors in their own past that may be influencing current issues in their lives. Once they understand what's causing their problems—including factors from their childhood—they move to a better position to find solutions. That's where you can help.

First, take some time to reflect upon your many successes as a parent. Try to remember the love and attention you lavished on your child, the special events that created lasting memories, the day-to-day rituals and playfulness that brought joy into your household.

Exercise

Write down some of these memories. Finish this sentence with all the thoughts it evokes for you:

It makes me feel gratified as a parent that I can remember

_____

_____

_____

_____

Keep this piece of writing close at hand as you embark on the less pleasant task of facing your unhappier memories.

Once again, try to go back to that place inside yourself where you can feel the unconditional love you felt for your young child. Savor the physical memory of holding and kissing your baby, playing with your toddler, and exchanging those warm looks and hugs over the years.

Now, let yourself remember the times when something got in the way of that unconditional love. Were there times when you were distracted by a life crisis of your own? Were you ever depressed or stressed to the point that you couldn't be emotionally present for your child? Were you overly critical of your child at those times when you were feeling down on yourself for some reason? Did you get carried away with your own emotions?

Exercise

One can't stay with these memories too long without feeling some sadness. Write down memories of how you felt, what you did, and what you said at these times. If you can, write an honest assessment of your parental lapses by completing this sentence:

It makes me feel sad to remember the times when I

_____

_____

_____

_____

Now, consider the times when you reacted with good parental skills to the inevitable misbehavior of your child. Remember the times when you refused to indulge in an angry response but calmly suggested a more appropriate course of action for your child, and later tried to find out what had caused your child to act out.

What was different about the times when you used poor parenting skills from the times when you used good parenting skills? What came into play from your own life that may have negatively influenced your treatment of your child? Which harsh reactions were similar to how you were treated by your own parents? Did you experience a lack of parental love yourself as a child? Or were these poor responses the result of other crises that drew your energy away from your child?

Exercise

Try to be honest with yourself and forgiving. Finish this sentence:

I did my best as a parent, but there were times when I was caught up with needs and problems of my own, including

_____

_____

_____

Once you make an honest assessment of your past parenting, you can begin to forgive yourself for the natural tendency to have been influenced by unhealthy social conventions, your own parents' shortcomings, and the various stresses you experienced during your child-rearing years. Then you can begin to look at the effects of your child-rearing practices on your adult child today and on your relationship together. You are helping yourself, your child, and the relationship the two of you share by recognizing emotional factors that shaped who you both are today.

The Relationship with Your Grown Child Today

The following questions may help you understand the dynamics of your relationship with your child.

Exercise

Does your child confide in you?

If the answer is "yes," you are in an excellent position to offer wisdom to your adult child to help with the present problem. If the answer is "no," you will have to find a way to re-establish feelings of mutual trust and respect before you can participate in an effective way in your adult child's life.

Anne

Anne's daughter shares intimate details of her life with Anne, even though Anne tends to be more guarded about her own confidences. Anne realizes that her daughter trusts her, but she doesn't want to shake that trust by criticizing her daughter's parenting skills. She believes she can find a way to communicate with her daughter in a nonthreatening way. She also believes that as long as she doesn't shake her daughter's trust, her daughter will probably value the insight.

Trust is not available in infinite quantities. We earn it, but we can also lose it, little by little or a lot at one time. In highly trusting relationships, we can afford to gamble a little by treading into uncharted territory. But, like Anne, it's wise to move cautiously into any subject area that might cause a withdrawal of trust.

Exercise

Do you think your child is happy to have had you as a parent?

_____

_____

If the answer is "yes," you already have a strong enough bond to deal with the common problems that come up with your adult child. If the answer is "no," there is probably resentment between the two of you that must be handled before you can be of true support to your adult child.

Mark

"*My daughter probably wishes she had a different parent, or maybe a couple of them. I was a single father and there's no doubt that my daughter grew up too fast, cooking and cleaning for her younger brothers. We didn't have much choice about that. I had to work, we couldn't afford household help, and she was the only one old enough to pitch in. I could have been more sensitive to her needs as a girl. I never intentionally mistreated her, but I realize now that I ignored messages from her. I suppose she was asking for limits, for respect. I teased her.*

"*She started picking 'macho' boyfriends who seemed to worship her femininity. I wish there'd been more information available to me about girls' needs. She needed someone around who was sensitive enough to figure out what she needed. If she'd had that, maybe then she would have picked a husband who treated her better.*"

If you suspect your child may feel some profound disappointment in you, then that may need to be handled before you can move forward. Often it's enough to acknowledge what you now see as lacking in your parenting skills and to assure your child that you'll try to be more sensitive from now on.

Exercise

Do you tiptoe as if walking on eggshells around your adult child, keeping a lid on your own thoughts or feelings so as not to create upset?

_____

_____

If the answer is "yes," your child probably feels anger and a sense of having been wronged, and more than likely that anger is negatively affecting many aspects of your child's life—and yours.

Lynn

"I am very, very careful about what I say to my son because at any time he might 'go off.' Now he's asking me for help with his life, and I've been afraid to demand that he get treatment for alcohol addiction. My own frustration is clear to me. I'm beginning to see that his anger may be a major factor in all of this. He did have some difficult experiences early in his life, including his father's death, his trouble at school, and his time in Vietnam.

"I refuse to blame myself for all his problems, but I can admit my role in them. I didn't give him the support he needed as a child to cope with all the troubles he has experienced. I am sorry about that, but do I have to continue paying for the rest of my life?"

Often when a grown child is angry, the parent also feels angry. In Lynn's case, her anger at being the "victim" of a troubled son was unexpressed until she became involved with Al-Anon. It helped to examine her own childhood and remember how she had avoided conflict. Her tiptoeing around was a sign that Lynn needed to set some limits with her son. As Lynn developed more self-respect, her anger began to dissipate and she was more open to loving.

Exercise

Does your adult child crave praise and attention, seeming unable to recognize the consequences of their actions?

_____

_____

If the answer is "yes," your child may have narcissistic tendencies, possibly due to past abandonment or neglect at some point in life, and could be making poor life choices as a result.

Tom

As Tom considered his daughter's plan to move home, he consciously recognized for the first time some lingering concerns about her lack of awareness about other people's needs. In proposing to move home, Amber talked only in terms of her own needs; she seemed unconscious of her parents as people with lives of their own. She had always been overly focused on her own desires. That might have been because Tom and his wife had been overprotective and had handled all her responsibilities growing up. Although they had done a lot "for" her, they hadn't done a lot "with" her to teach self-responsibility, nor had they required her to take any responsibility in the household. She'd become accustomed to being indulged and perhaps still needed some lessons in how to participate in the real give-and-take that marks healthy relationships.

Exercise

Do your children keep you at arm's length?

_____

_____

If so, it's possible they considered you either intrusive or out of reach when they were younger; they may be continuing to assert boundaries because they fear you may either take over or disappear. In this case, it will be very difficult for you to give advice or help in any way unless you can rebuild a relationship with clear boundaries.

Jake

"My daughter seems to want to keep us at a geographic distance. It's true that there were uncomfortable times when she was growing up. I was working a lot, including times when I should have been taking her places or spending time with her at home. When I was with her, I guess I pushed too far. I didn't always respect her privacy. I remember one time when she was about twelve, I read aloud from a little journal she kept. There wasn't anything really secret in there, but she was really upset. If I talk to her about all that, and give her a couple-of-decades-late apology, maybe we can start talking about some of the ground rules if we end up living closer to each other now."

It's possible to overcome experiences that may have eroded trust in the past. In Jake's case, his daughter saw him as invading her privacy when she was a child, while he failed to get involved in her school and sports activities because he was too busy. Jake does have a lot to offer his daughter now, but he will need to prove that, step-by-step, starting with honoring small agreements and perhaps sharing some revelations about himself.

Exercise

Do you feel jealous of your child's good fortune, freedom, or abilities?

_____

_____

If the answer is "yes," your child might see you as a martyr and be nervous about having you around, because you might bring a cloud of judgment over their life.

Kathryn

Kathryn wishes she'd had some of the luxury her daughter enjoys. Kathryn and her husband had to struggle with budgets and work schedules. But now her daughter, the wife of a fabulously wealthy doctor, devotes herself to being a wife, mother, and an object of beauty, seemingly unconcerned about her husband's attention to other women. Kathryn loves her daughter and wants only the best for her, but she also judges her daughter harshly, talking to her friends about her daughter's shallow lifestyle and "cheating" husband.

Subconscious jealousy can create hostility. Usually, once parents recognize this in themselves (and it's often embarrassing to admit it), they can get over it, perhaps by developing in their own lives what they envy about their child's.

Exercise

Do members of your family talk behind one another's back, trading information that was given in confidence?

_____

_____

If not, there is more likely to be a foundation of trust, and your adult child will probably feel safe opening up to you. If so, your adult child likely won't trust you enough to talk openly or be "totally known" by you, perhaps fearing criticism and family ridicule.

Sally

Sally's other kids talk behind her daughter Michelle's back about Michelle's ne'er-do-well boyfriend. It's as if they enjoy the "ain't it awful" conversations about poor Michelle. Michelle was a premature baby, isolated for the first three months of her life. In a way, she never fit into the family or felt as though she belonged. She didn't receive a lot of nurturing. Now that Michelle has found someone who needs her, Sally is coming to terms with how the family dynamics may have influenced Michelle's choices.

Family gossip can provide a form of bonding, albeit an unhealthy one, for those in the loop. But the practice carries a high cost. The connections are tenuous among those inside the loop, and the odd-one-out can feel dangerously isolated. Parents who provide wise leadership in their families will set an example by refusing to talk about others when they aren't there—unless it's a brainstorming, positive, goal-oriented discussion to avert a crisis.

Exercise

Are you hard to please?

If your child perceives you as difficult to please, they may have grown up questioning your love (and, often, hard-to-please parents grew up with the same worries about one or both of their own parents). This situation can result in your child's continuing dependency long after entering adulthood. When parents are overly critical, children become accustomed to looking for love and approval, making themselves other-oriented instead of relying on their internal resources for a sense of self-worth. Being hard to please also can make communication difficult because the child worries about being "criticized" when parents are trying to "help." In this situation, a bond of acceptance must be established before a parent can begin working with an adult child on a solution to current problems.

Paula

After the experience of being obviously ignored by her visiting daughter when Paula tried to provide time-management advice, Paula recognizes the way her kids' eyes frequently glaze over when she gets together with them, and she suspects they use the answering machine to screen out calls from her. As she became aware that they are probably trying to avoid her opinions, Paula began to think about the high standards she had held up to her children. Something had been lost in their family with the constant striving for achievement and order when they were young. Now, she wishes they'd had more time to feel relaxed and cozy.

She has been trying to make changes in her own life, enjoying herself and becoming more relaxed in her conversations and visits with her children. Still, it's hard to let go of wanting to help them live "better" lives. But she sees the irony in how the more she rides them, the less inclined they are to hear what she's trying to say.

Being a parent with high standards can be habit-forming, but usually you can tell when your perfectionism is getting in the way of your relationships. If it is getting in the way, you need to relax—both with yourself and with your children—as Paula did by attending a women's retreat where she was able to talk candidly about life as a perfectionist.

Exercise

Do you typically withdraw into yourself when there is a crisis? Or have you had long periods of illness? Or did you distance yourself from your child due to divorce or other problems?

_____

_____

Beth

Beth was a quiet child who read voraciously, loved puzzles, and was a born problem solver, that is, when it came to mathematical problems. But she was never much of a "people person." Her husband left her and their young son in part because he felt isolated in their relationship. Beth had tried to open up and become more relaxed, but her nature was reserved and introverted.

As a single mother, she had seldom discussed emotions with her son. They were comfortable together, but, looking back, she sees herself as having been emotionally inaccessible. She doesn't have an easy way now to reach out to her son, as he seems to be growing further away from her in his adult life. It helps, though, to have a clearer view of how her personality may have contributed to the present distance with her son. She's beginning to understand some of the causes of the barriers between them.

Kathryn

"I was an at-home mom, so it never occurred to me that I was withdrawing from my children. But in retrospect, I was much more 'myself' outside the family unit, with secret relationships that drained some of my love and energy away from my kids.

"Now my daughter has everything she wants in terms of material things, but she is emotionally needy, and that's one reason why her husband's flirtations are so devastating to me. I wonder if she sensed my emotional distance when she was small? Maybe I'm partially to blame for her marriage to a man who seems to have emotionally abandoned her. Will it help if I tell her about my own affairs?"

When parents are reserved, children sometimes get the message that they are unwanted. It can be a source of reassurance, at any age, for someone to hear their parents say that they may have failed to express the love they felt over the years. It is not necessary to "confess" about one's past problems, however. Kathryn's marriage did not end in divorce, and she has realized there is probably no reason for her children to know about her past affairs.

Kathryn

Instead of focusing on self-blame for her past adultry, Kathryn shifted her focus to the deeper meaning of her past behavior in hopes of better understanding her daughter's current plight. Like her daughter, Kathryn felt unfulfilled in her marriage when her children were small, but was in denial about the problems. Instead of confronting the issues in her own marriage, Kathryn had turned to other men for a distraction. Kathryn's daughter seemed to be absorbed in her social life and role as a mother perhaps partially as a distraction from her current marital problems.

As Kathryn looked for similarities in her daughter's situation and her own situation years ago, she realized that both of them probably had low self-esteem. They were inclined to look outward rather than inward for affirmation. What had happened to her daughter's love of painting and other artistic pursuits? For that matter, what had happened to her own creativity, her past joy in writing poetry?

After giving deep thought to the matter, Kathryn felt that both she and her daughter needed better outlets to express themselves. She did some research and found there was an upcoming retreat on women's creativity in a resort town roughly halfway between her home and her daughter's. She called and suggested to her daughter that they attend together. Her daughter could bring the children and a nanny. It took sone fast talking, but Kathryn convinced her daughter that it was always a good idea for a woman to have a hobby. Recognizing her daughter's tendency toward people pleasing, Kathryn suggested that her daughter might enjoy having some of her own artwork to auction off at the next fund-raiser for her children's private school. She sensed her daughter's lack of confidence about resuming her art, but ultimately her daughter agreed to attend the workshop. Kathryn offered to pay, but her daughter insisted on covering her own expenses. By the end of the conversation, Kathryn could hear a hint of excitement in her daughter's voice. It sounded like her daughter welcomed the opportunity to get away and have some time with Kathryn.

Exercise

Have you looked to your own children for personal support over the years, confiding in them and depending on them to give your life meaning?

If, due to your own unmet needs, you have placed unreasonable demands on your children for kinship, they may fear your dependence upon them. Sometimes taking care of yourself—and letting go of needing your child, at least for the time being—is the best route for everyone.

Rosa

"Because I had my daughter so young, and I had such a bad marriage, I found myself completely wrapped up in her. The closeness was a source of warmth and comfort for both of us, I thought at the time, but looking back I may have depended on her too much, at the price of my own growth—and hers. In a way, we grew up together. Everything was 'we,' and I lived too much through her. Now she seems so rejecting. Perhaps one thing I can do is acknowledge to her that my own youth was a factor in expecting too much from her as a child."

Recognizing a past pattern of enmeshment can help both the parent and the child concentrate on more appropriate ways to be together as two adults.

Exercise

Are you a worrier whose parenting was marked by overprotection and an inability to let go?

The overprotective parent may have unwittingly humiliated a child and stood in the way of healthy growth toward autonomy. The result can be stifling for both parent and child. In these families, parents of adult children must ask themselves if their current desire to help is an extension of an overprotective history. They must guard against giving the kind of "help" that undermines autonomy. People should be given the respect to solve their own problems whenever they can.

Richard

When their children were growing up, Richard and his wife were fearful for their kids' safety, imposing strict rules about where they could go and when. They read newspaper accounts to their children

*about violent events, and warned them about the dangers of life. They
worried when the kids rode their bicycles a few blocks from home and
when they went to dances as teenagers.*

*Now their son seems uncomfortable about leaving his children
with anyone but their grandparents. Within a couple of years, the
grandkids will be going off to school, and it's time for their parents to
begin trusting people outside the family to watch them. Richard and his
wife see their overprotectiveness being perpetuated in the next
generation. At the same time, they may be unwittingly undermining
their son and daughter-in-law's need to help their children feel safe
outside of the extended family.*

If you've inadvertently undermined your kids' sense of autonomy
when they were younger, you can't go back in time and give them the
opportunities to gain a sense of confidence about the world. But it is possible to express confidence in your children now and stop taking care of them
in inappropriate ways. For Richard, that may mean giving up the role of
primary child-care provider with an expression of confidence that his son
and daughter-in-law can find a good situation for their kids and that the
kids will do just fine.

Recognizing how your past patterns have resulted in problems with
expressing love, respect, or trust can make you feel regretful. But it's pre-
cisely the information you need to renew your bond. Of course, you can't go
back and re-create healthy parenting practices that you wish you'd used in
the past. The formative years are over, and much of your child's personality
and many of your child's attitudes are already shaped. But many well-documented studies of human development have demonstrated that personal
growth continues well into adulthood, so take heart. It is possible to have a
healthy influence in your child's life, demonstrating by your own behavior
that change is possible. If you can take what you've learned from examining
your past parenting practices and share that information with your child,
you can serve as a role model for change.

Sibling Rivalry

If you have more than one child, you are probably well aware of the phenomenon of sibling rivalry. Perhaps you expected they would "outgrow"
it—and maybe they have—but competition among siblings often continues
well into adulthood. Some people go to their graves with old resentments
toward a sister or brother.

Rivalry can stem from a number of factors:

1. The real or perceived favor of one gender over the other in a
   family

2. Each child may have different talents and abilities; parents may demonstrate more appreciation of some talents than others.

3. The natural tendency of any group to form alliances

4. Family politics that often result in making a scapegoat of one member who is outspoken, troubled, or withdrawn

Old hurts between siblings may seem to be healed, only to be felt again at unexpected moments, often at family gatherings, over anything from the inequitable distribution of gifts or heirlooms to a perceived difference in attention to grandchildren. Sibling rivalry is pervasive and deep. No wonder the Smothers Brothers elicited belly laughs for decades with their "Mother always did like you best" routine. As the Smothers Brothers can attest, humor helps. And so does having enough love to discuss and work through differences. Dick Smothers talked to a reporter from the *Santa Rosa Press Democrat* in 1996 about how he and his brother had gone through counseling to keep the lines of communication open between them and to ensure the future ongoing success of their beloved comedy act. In the following story, you will see how Connie's son was a victim of less healthy sibling rivalry, which was never really discussed among family members.

Connie

Connie and her husband remembered the strong rivalry between their two daughters and their son. Their son was bright and sensitive as a child, but that brought teasing at home and at school. At the time, Connie and her husband thought their job was to "toughen him up." In hindsight, he should have received support and perhaps counseling to help him develop coping strategies. Connie wishes they had intervened to prevent their daughters from excessively teasing their son, who was probably feeling lonely and confused.

Few parents have the magic necessary to make sibling rivalry simply disappear, but you can help by trying to remember how it manifested when your children were younger—recognizing ways in which you could have handled it better—and encouraging humor. You can find ways to demonstrate your awareness that the bond between family members is more important than conflicts that occasionally flash up.

Seeing the Connections

Exercise

Take a piece of paper and do the following free-writing exercise to explore your family system. First, think back to your family tree. Pretend you're having a therapy session with your kids, your parents, and other important people in your entire extended family. Imagine yourselves connected by ribbons that you have tied among yourselves. Imagine what happens when one moves closer or farther away. See the ways in which you are all interdependent.

Now write down words or phrases that come to mind when you consider how your behavior influenced your children and the way your parents' behavior influenced you. Use pictures, symbols, or anything else that appears on the paper when you think about the complicated relationships in your family.

What influenced your parenting when your children were growing up? What would you do differently today? How is your presence important in your grown children's lives? What do you want to give? What do you want to get in return? Let the words flow:

_____

_____

_____

_____

_____

_____

_____

_____

Michael

"My background of poverty contributed enormously to my value system. In retrospect, I focused too much on austerity with my children, trying to get them to appreciate everything and not waste resources. Now as I see how my son overindulges his kids, I realize that my efforts backfired. I have to forgive myself for doing what I thought was best, which was a natural result of my own upbringing.

"Still, the net effect was that my kids may have felt deprived because it was so hard for me to be generous. Now that I'm beginning to see the pattern, I'd like to make things right with my kids and with my grandkids. I want my kids to know I always loved them, even though I didn't give them things. Perhaps that knowledge could help my son become less obsessed with giving his kids 'everything.' I want for my

grandkids to see beyond things and appreciate others, and to learn to be civilized and loving people. And I want to be one of the recipients of their love."

Michael began to realize that material objects had long been a potent symbol for his family, negative in the past due to poverty, and negative in the present, perhaps due to any overcompensation he inadvertently might have caused. With this awareness, he is more prepared to come up with a better way to handle discomfort over the "spoiling" of his grandchildren.

It's easy to become immobilized by guilt. And it's equally easy to ignore unpleasant past experiences. But if you are to become an active influence, loving and supportive, in your grown children's lives, it's best to find a middle ground. You can be truthful with yourself about the past, without minimizing or overestimating the effect of your mistakes.

In order to let go of self-blame, you can look at the complex factors that caused you to be the kind of parent you were. You are a product of your family system the same way that your children are products of theirs. Knowledge about the powerful effects families have on individuals will help you see yourself as part of a system. Forgiving yourself will free you to strengthen your relationships. Sometimes, you also may need to forgive your child.

Forgiving Your Child

Even though it's hard to admit, many parents have been hurt by their children. For people like Rosa and Lynn, the betrayal is clear and continues with disrespectful or burdensome behavior by a child who wants to use the parent as an emotional punching bag or crutch. For someone like Tom, the betrayal is more subtle: The grown child simply fails to respect the parents' needs because she wants what she wants, allowing bad feelings to linger.

As you get to a place of heightened self-awareness, you can see how blame can get in the way of finding a mutually satisfying solution. Emotional matters often don't respond to reason. It's a major breakthrough simply to realize your resentments and to wish to forgive. Then you can take steps toward letting go of your resentments.

Exercise

As an exercise, write on a blank piece of paper a few words that describe your issues with your grown child. Read your words. Then, fold the paper twice and literally burn it in the flame of a candle. This action can serve as a symbolic reminder that you want to let go of your grudges.

It's hard work to acknowledge what part your parenting practices played in the life of your grown child. But it can free up your energy for developing more intimacy with your family.

When parents identify and communicate the ways they let their children down over the years, they can help their children see more clearly what they, themselves, need to overcome as adults. You can recognize the truth and share it. This kind of honesty is an immeasurable gift, bringing as much to the giver as to the receiver.

Chapter 6 will offer you a few reminders, and some new ideas, about how to make the most of communication with your grown children.

CHAPTER 6

Beyond Advice: Enlightened Communication

At the end, truth is the only thing worth having: it's more thrilling than love, more joyful and more passionate.

— Colette

The most exhausting thing in my life is being insincere.

—Anne Morrow Lindberg

When children are young, their words often tumble out in a rush of enthusiasm as they tell their parents what they see, think, and feel. "Watch me! Listen to me!" they seem to be saying, over and over in so many different ways. They want their parents to know them and accept them for who they are. And, if they feel abundantly loved and accepted throughout childhood, they may continue open communication with their parents in adulthood.

It takes a near saint to be constantly available to truly hear others, whenever they speak. The people considered the wisest of our time often affect others profoundly not just because of what they say, but also because of how they *respond* to what others say. It has been said about Gandhi and others that they "made you feel as though you were the only person in the room, that they had all the time in the world for you."

Recognizing Past Barriers to Good Communication

Few of us are saints. And, as we've acknowledged before in this book, parental love is imperfect. Sad as it is to admit, most of us didn't always respond appropriately when our young children wanted our attention. If there are barriers in your communication with your child today, probably there were times in the past when you failed to listen carefully when your child wanted to be heard. However, you shouldn't blame yourself entirely for the communication problems you have with your grown child. Today your grown child shares responsibility for the quality of your interactions. But you can set the tone for renewed openness and authenticity in your communication by recognizing barriers from the past.

Look once again at the portrait of your past parenting practices in chapter 5. What got in the way of open, loving communication? It's not pleasant, but it's useful to dig up memories of the times when you didn't listen carefully or communicate clearly with your young one. It's a step toward re-establishing a trusting connection with your grown child today.

Did you frequently:

- Pretend you were listening while thinking about work or other activities?

- Think up your response while your child was telling you something?

- Turn away while your child was talking to concentrate on reading the paper, cooking, cleaning, repairing something?

- Lie about your activities when your child challenged you?

- Roll your eyes and say:
  "I've heard this a hundred times before."
  "I said 'no' and that's it. No discussion."
  "Because I said so."
  "I'm an adult so I can do ____. You're a child so you can't."
  "Not now. I have to work."

Such tuning-out mechanisms are fairly typical, but they get in the way of loving communication. If you often tuned out your children when they were young, they may still think of you as someone who does not have enough time or interest to hear what they are saying.

Sometimes communication difficulties go back generations and may seem almost a part of the family DNA. It can be a challenge to see, much less to get past, counterproductive patterns.

Since we usually have blind spots for our own failures, a good way to see any problems you may have had in the past is to analyze the feedback you typically received years ago. Try to remember the words your children spoke years ago, so that you can understand what communication barriers you have to overcome now. Did you hear these words from your children?

- I just can't talk to you.
  (You seem distant, unconcerned about me.)

- You never listen.
  (You're more interested in your agenda than hearing what I have to say.)

- I wish you'd leave me alone.
  (You're too intrusive. Give me space. Talk to me when I'm ready.)

- You're always too busy.
  (I don't feel like a priority in your life.)

- I was just kidding, why can't you have a sense of humor?
  (You're too uptight. Lighten up. It will be easier.)

- I'm afraid to talk to you.
  (Things you've said or done in the past have hurt me so much that I do not want to risk communication.)

- You sound like a tape recorder.
  (You say the same things over and over again.)

- I don't trust you.
  (You've betrayed my confidence or used my words against me.)

Now let's move to the sunny side of "memory lane," and recall the times when your son or daughter expressed trust in you and had a feeling of connection.

- What do you think about . . . ?
  (Your opinion is important to me.)

- Tell me a story about when you were younger.
  (I'm interested in you.)

- Know what happened today?
  (I want to share my experiences with you.)

- Did you ever have something like this happen to you?
  (Your experiences help me understand my own experiences.)

- I love it when you talk about. . . .
  (Talking to you is enlightening.)

- I can tell you anything.
  (I trust you.)

Consider both the positive and negative aspects of your past communication techniques, then clear the decks and realize you can start fresh. You're developing new skills that are more appropriate for enriching relationships with your adult child.

As our colleague, management expert Richard Anstruther, says, when it comes to any new skill, there's a learning curve that goes from being unconsciously incompetent, to consciously incompetent, to consciously competent, to unconsciously competent. That is, you begin with no idea you're doing anything wrong, to knowing something's wrong, to developing better skills; ultimately you end up being so good that you don't have to think anymore about it.

You can't go back and change the past, but you can learn some new communication skills, outlined in this chapter, that will let your children know that you have a profound interest in their words. If you practice good communication, you will serve as a role model for your grown children, while soothing your own spirit—knowing you're doing the best you can. No one learns how to be a parent of adults automatically. It takes some effort. And you're making the commitment to do it.

Keeping Your Eye on the Prize

Learning new communication techniques is hard work, and it helps to have a clear idea of your goal. You're less likely to get bogged down in frustration or power struggles if you keep in mind the result you want to achieve. Before sitting down to talk with your grown child, consider your goal.

Tom

"I want my daughter to feel loved and supported, knowing she has a place in the family forever. But I want to find a way to let her know that we believe that as an adult she can handle her own life. I don't want her to confuse being dependent with being loved. And I want my wife and myself to enjoy freedom from responsibility for our grown daughter."

Don

"My goal is to convince my daughter that we want to be with her and her new family. I want her to know I accept her as a lesbian and that we will not be watching her every move as the mother of a son in this unusual arrangement. I want to tell her how proud I am of her for becoming a doctor. She's beautiful, brilliant, and hardworking, and perhaps I have neglected to acknowledge all of that. I hope to play a role in her and her son's life."

Exercise

State your goal in the communication with your grown child:

_____

_____

_____

_____

_____

Evolving Your Communication Style

People who read books like this tend to be open to new ways of expanding their repertoire of behaviors in order to enhance the quality of their relationships. Chances are you're the kind of person who already has some background in the fundamentals of good communication. Thus, the ideas presented here probably will serve to remind you of what you already know.

Over the years, you may have worked on your communication skills during your child-rearing time, in your marriage, or at work. Each time, you adapted those skills for the situation. The challenge now is to apply that knowledge to your parent–adult child relationship. As you read the following list, picture yourself using these skills in a conversation with your grown child.

Do	Don't
Set up an agreed-upon time	Suddenly begin conversation
Make eye contact	Look down or around the room
Concentrate on hearing	Concentrate on being heard
Describe your experience	Blame
Share feelings of pain	Keep a stiff upper lip
Have realistic expectations	Be a perfectionist
Begin sentences with "I . . ."	Begin sentences with "You . . ."
Perceive emotions	Focus only on words spoken
Maintain respect	Show exasperation
Allow the other to speak	Interrupt
Accept uncomfortable words	React quickly
Respect the other's pace	Demand or push for information
Express confusion	Demand answers
Be prepared with a clear message	Talk on and on
Expect the unexpected	Be tied to a certain result

Do	Don't
Be open to the other's agenda	Direct the conversation
Seek to understand	Judge
Talk less than half the time	Lecture
Start fresh	Recycle old gripes
Remember deep love	Close off emotions

It Takes Two

Obviously there are some occasions when a grown child is being manipulative in their communication with you. Some grown kids who refuse to grow up will try to make parents feel guilty. You can proceed with fair and loving communication techniques even when your grown child is not doing so. It won't help to accuse: "There you go again, using put-downs to manipulate me!" But you can keep focused on your goal and refuse to allow yourself to be drawn into a counterproductive exchange.

Giving Advice

Perhaps the most famous piece of parental advice is in William Shakespeare's *Hamlet*, when Laertes is preparing to set sail for France, and his father, Polonius, launches forth on a soliloquy filled with timeless and profound truths as relevant today as when they were written. It ends with the memorable words, "This above all, to thine own self be true. And it must follow as the night the day, Thou canst not then be false to any man."

The speech imparts wisdom that has resonated for centuries for millions of people. But, for all we know, all that advice went in one ear and out the other for its intended recipient.

The rest of us may have understood what Polonius had to say. But one can't help but wonder: Was Laertes really listening? The toughest audience of all is your own children. Others may consider you profound and even brilliant; your own kids may have built up an immunity to your attempts to inoculate them with your hard-won knowledge about life.

Is there anything more frustrating than watching your offspring make a mistake that might have been prevented if only they'd known something—something you could have told them, if only you'd thought they'd have listened; or, worse yet, something you did tell them but they got into trouble because they didn't take your advice? It's particularly frustrating when you've made the same mistake and you know the consequences. Coincidence? Hardly. Of course, grown children make the same mistakes as their parents did. They learned how to live by watching us.

Hopefully, you gave your kids the tools to do things for themselves. Throughout the years, you were balancing their need for help with their need to figure things out for themselves. Obviously, you don't tell a toddler to put the round peg in the round hole if it robs him of the opportunity of figuring it out on his own. But what if he's tried the square hole fifteen times and could use just a little nudge that would move him in the right direction?

Similarly, it undermines their autonomy to tell grown kids how to live their lives. On the other hand, sometimes they need more information than they have to make wise decisions. Especially when the stakes are high—involving physical safety, financial security, or emotional matters—it's almost impossible for parents to sit back and watch quietly without speaking up.

How much advice you can give, and how you go about it, is largely a function of the kind of relationship you have with your grown child. If you're close enough, you can set some ground rules—perhaps have an agreement that you ask permission of each other before giving advice. Having these rules opens communication and prevents advice from being perceived as criticism.

For example, when Eileen Clegg took a car trip cross-country with her mother, Iris Ridgway, they agreed that "back-seat driving" was permitted. With all the unexpected occurrences that can happen during long hours on the road, they decided it was safer if they both felt free to speak up. At first, it was a little annoying, but because they had a clear agreement that driving advice was okay, their irritation with each other wore off pretty quickly. As it turned out, there were a couple of instances when the passenger's observations helped the driver avoid trouble.

The experience of what Iris and Eileen called "driving by committee" opened the door for a lot of discussion on the subject of advice giving. One of the destinations on the trip was a family reunion in Minnesota. It was a natural place to continue the discussion. One cousin talked about a rule on her branch of the family tree: "Mom tells us her opinions, and we do what we think is best. And that's fine with her." Openness and humor can create an environment for the free exchange of ideas, without the the advice giver's usual prickly attachments to the end results.

In Eileen's family, a shared sense of humor helps ease the awkwardness of advice giving and taking, as do clear ground rules that have developed over time. The idea for this book grew out of a particularly difficult time in the family, when Iris was anguished over one of her grown children's crises and wished she had spoken up years earlier when the signs of trouble began. "That's it!" Iris announced. "From now on I'm meddling!" It was half-serious, half-humorous, but that comment gave rise to a lot of talk about how the family could establish a supportive network while avoiding intrusion. It's a continuing conversation: How does a parent walk the line, providing advice without meddling in the adult child's life? In relationships where there are sufficient love and warmth, people enjoy a sort of emotional cushion. They don't have to be quite as careful about their words, knowing that others feel comfortable and understand that their intentions are good.

Michael

When Michael realized that his grandchildren's excessive materialism rankled him because of his own childhood deprivation, he decided it was time to treat himself. He planned a drive to the country with his wife and signed them up for massages, a hot-air balloon ride, and dinner at a five-star restaurant. "That's going to cost a lot," his grandson said when Michael talked about the plans. Michael laughed, "Especially for an old scrooge like me. Got any money?" His grandson said, "No, because I'm following your advice to save it." Michael chuckled, "I think we're learning from each other about what to do with money."

Show, Don't Tell

Unless you have a completely "clear" and mutually accepting relationship, where your grown child is convinced that you are coming from a place of love with no underlying agenda, it's usually a waste of breath to give advice. But there are many other ways to share your wisdom with another person: The best "advice" is to be an example. The "do as I say not as I do" attitude unfortunately is widespread, and it does not work. Regardless of your children's age, they probably subconsciously ask themselves "What would mom do?" or "What would dad do?" in this situation. They will remember your actions more than your words. If they respect you, they're likely to incorporate your ideas into their actions. If you see your adult child struggling with a problem, you might try telling an anecdote from your own experience as a way to give them valuable information.

Beth

Beth recalled an incident with her own mother-in-law and shared it with her son. "I often felt inadequate around your father's mother because she was so skilled in domestic matters and I was bookish and unskilled at cooking and sewing. One Christmas she came over with these beautiful handmade Christmas stockings and looked at the dime-store ones I had hanging on the hearth. I told her, 'You must think I'm so incompetent.' I was surprised when she told me that she had always felt awed by me because of all my education. That really cleared the air between us."

Richard

Realizing that his son probably had some anxiety about finding good child care, Richard went back over thirty years in his own memory to when he and his wife got their first babysitter to go out for an evening. He shared the memory with his son: "We were so nervous. You were crying when we left. 'He'll be fine the minute you leave,' the babysitter told us. We didn't believe her. We got about a block away, then turned back. When we walked up the steps to the house, we could hear you inside laughing. We were relieved, but your mom and I found ourselves wondering what you found so funny. We wished we could share the moment. Turns out we probably missed you a lot more than you missed us!"

Paula

"I finally gave up on the idea that I could manage my grown kids' lives, even though I'm sure I could do a pretty good job of it. Seriously, I know that it's essential that I give up any attempts to be controlling. I really want to be done with that aspect of my personality. It's fun surprising them with the more carefree approach I'm taking these days . If they mention a problem, I tell them a story. Recently my daughter was complaining about feeling so rushed and always eating out, often at fast-food restaurants. So, I told her that when I was working full-time, I struggled with that, too, and that's when I taught her how to cook! Her first recipe was macaroni and cheese, but now it's called 'Pasta Alfredo.'"

Telling stories with humor is one way to help your kids *see* something that you believe will help them. Other suggestions are to:

- See a movie together that has similarities to the situation.

- Suggest a novel or magazine article that has pertinent information.

- Watch and talk about a TV program that had a theme common to the issue at hand.

- Tell them an inspirational quote.

Writing a Letter

The written word is powerful. Marriages have been saved by letters written from the heart that revealed deep feelings, unexpressed needs, secret longings, and love. What these letters had in common was that they not only shared the deep convictions of the writer but asked the other to share their feelings in return.

For a letter to have such a healing effect, it must come from an open place, not judging or hostile, but inviting deeper connection. Many of these letters have asked for forgiveness. Such letters are less frequently shared between parents and children, but when they are they can work miracles.

Sally

"As I watched my daughter getting deeper and deeper in a relationship that seemed to drain her and not give much back, I began to hold her in my mind when I did my Transcendental Meditation exercises. Slowly, I began remembering more about my daughter as a baby, premature in the hospital and then a stranger to me when she finally came home three months later. Her brothers and sisters were annoyed with her crying and delicacy and didn't treat her warmly. And my bonding with her was shaky. She had trouble fitting into the family. At the time, I was just unaware of what was happening. Now it causes me great sadness. I'd never talked to her about her infancy, so I decided to write her a letter.

"'I want to tell you some things from when you were small, things I'm sad about and wish I could go back and change for you and for me. It was hard for me to get to know you when you were a baby because they kept you in an incubator in the hospital and, back then, they didn't allow moms to nurse or hold the babies. You and I didn't really have a chance to develop the kind of attachment that mothers and babies need with one another. When you were a small child, you may have felt that I turned away from you, that I was impatient, or that I didn't give you the hugs and nurturing I gave your brothers and sisters. Something held me back. I'm sorry, but I'm here for you now and always. Love, Mom.'"

Look for a Good Opening

Sometimes parents want to communicate information that is truly unwelcome. Unless there is a crisis or dangerous problem at hand, it's usually best to refrain from offering your opinions about a grown child's life. However, there may be occasions when your grown children recognize problems they have, and they may show a glimmer of willingness to discuss a subject that previously has been off-limits. When such opportunities to provide guidance arise, you might offer suggestions in a way that is supportive and nonjudgmental.

Michael

Michael recognized that it would be a communication disaster to blurt out his concerns, because of his long-simmering annoyance over his grandchildren's spoiled behavior. He had begun talking with his son about past family issues, and found ways to gently urge his grandkids to take some responsibility when they were visiting his home. He had decided not to say anything about his son's child-rearing practices. But as Michael grew more relaxed around his son's family, his son began opening up about some of his own concerns about the kids.

The opening for Michael to enter the discussion came one day when his son lamented "My kids are having trouble making friends, they just don't seem to get along well with other kids for very long." Michael showed interest and his son continued talking. Then, his son looked up at the ceiling and said, "Have you ever dealt with this kind of thing before?" Michael had already done some research, so he was prepared with some ideas about encouraging kids to take more responsibility. "You know," Michael said, "I just read something about how doing household chores can help kids feel more competent and part of things. It can be a confidence booster." His son nodded thoughtfully as though he got the connection between responsibility and social development. The next time Michael saw his grandsons, they were complaining about having to do yard work. That was progress, from Michael's perspective.

Asking Questions

In those gut-wrenching situations when a parent observes a serious problem brewing in the life of a grown child but has determined that it would be inappropriate or damaging to the relationship to bring it up, the carefully constructed question can be useful. Giving someone the third degree doesn't work. That would be meddling. But a neutrally posed query may start people thinking about a problem they may be trying to ignore.

This is not in the category of intervention. When the problems are serious or health-threatening, sometimes you have to speak up even if your child doesn't listen. But the subtle questioning technique can be applied when you see something that is worrisome but not dangerous. Think carefully before asking, and try to limit your query to a single question. Find a window of opportunity, and try to be casual.

Anne

Anne was having lunch with her daughter when, at a neighboring table, a father began nagging one of his youngsters to hurry and tie his shoes. The more insistent the father became, the more difficulty the child seemed to have. "This isn't rocket science. We're talking about tying your shoe," the father yelled. Anne made a point of quietly drawing her daughter's attention to the interaction. "That poor child is trying his best. Don't you think his father is making it more difficult for him?" Anne asked. Her daughter just shrugged uncomfortably and seemed to go into a reverie. The next time she saw her daughter and grandson, her daughter seemed a bit more patient and gentle with her child.

Atonement

In situations where lines of communication are in serious disrepair, it's likely that you'll need to take responsibility for your part of the problem and look to the past to define and acknowledge it. Atonement is more than apologizing. The word "atonement," first used in a religious sense, literally means "at-one-ment," or being at one with God or another person, according to Wilfred Funk's *Word Origins*. It means to become reconciled.

In relationships, to atone is to put yourself in the other's place and imagine how they felt when you hurt them. You try to almost become that person so that you can experience what they have experienced. You can lead them gently back to the pain and help to heal it.

The formula for atonement is to:

- Tell the truth.

- State in detail what you did.

- Share your view of what your child must have felt at the time.

- Promise that you won't do it again.

- Say that you're sorry.

- Ask how you can make amends.

It often takes a crisis before one has the opportunity to atone for the past. In Jake's case, it was the frustration he felt in the face of his daughter's coolness to engage in any discussion about his moving closer to her when he retired. He was forced to look back at the factors that had contributed to the current awkwardness, and found himself remembering the times he had let her down when she was a girl. He thought about his past breaches of trust, like when he read her diary. It was painful for him to think about his mistakes, but he realized that she might resent his turning to her now to fill an empty place in his life, when he had failed to meet her needs in the past. He wanted to reassure her of his love and his motives.

Jake

Jake's desire for open communication caused him anxiety, as well as his wife and daughter. No one was familiar with this facet of his personality, and it threw the family into a tizzy.

He was nervous about how and where to have a "real talk" with his daughter but finally scheduled a visit. He made the visit seem casual by coordinating it with a meeting in her town involving his new consulting business, which was a way to make some extra money during his retirement. He stayed at a motel in his daughter's town instead of at her house, spent Saturday afternoon with his grandkids, and took his daughter out to lunch on Sunday. He said he had something to say to her that wouldn't take long, and then he said to her what he had considered saying for a long time.

"I've been thinking about the time I wasn't there when your basketball team won the championship, even though I bragged to all my friends about it. I wasn't one of those dads who took you and your friends to the mall. A lot of times I wasn't even home for dinner. You must have felt less loved than your friends whose dads were more available. Then, when I was home, I tried to make up for lost time by jumping right in, sometimes in the wrong way. It must have made you feel terrible when I read your diary that time. I'm sorry about that and wish I could go back and do some things differently. At least we have some good memories of fishing!

"Anyway, your mom and I have a lot of possibilities for the future. We have a solid financial base, and that's even if my new consulting business doesn't bring in much. I thought you should know that we're financially secure.

"You know we've been thinking about moving closer to you and your family. We'd love to spend more time with you and the kids, and maybe have the kids come over after school instead of going to day care on some days. We have a year or so to decide, but maybe sometime we can talk about the possibilities. Either way, I hope you know how much I love you."

His daughter avoided his eyes while he was talking. Afterward she looked at him oddly and said, "I've never heard you talk like this before." Jake was crushed, feeling that he had made a terrible mistake with his candor. He hated whining, and that's how he'd sounded to himself. It was so uncomfortable.

After an awkward silence, Jake asked her if she had anything to say to him. She shook her head. But when they walked outside she seemed warmer, taking his arm when they crossed the street. She invited him over to the house that evening. Over dinner, she talked with animation about the children's activities, her work, and life in their small town. Jake was glad he'd made the effort to talk with her.

Mark

To his daughter Mark said, "Your brother told me about one time when you came home as a preteen and said it didn't feel like a home to you. He told me how the two of you would cut pictures out of magazines and make collages about the type of family you longed for. I'm sorry I didn't understand your unhappiness, that I belittled your

*requests for privacy, and ignored your need for a bedroom of your own. I
am aware that you may be suffering now and I want to help support
you. Will you forgive me for my past immaturity?"*

You can't expect your child to instantly become a willing receiver of
your communication, no matter how good your skills become. You may
have several false starts before you actually "come out with it." And it could
take months or even years before you develop a clear two-way line of interaction. But getting started can be a relief to everyone.

Taking an Easy Approach to Tough Subjects

Following are some suggestions for easing the strain of a difficult conversation:

- Keep it simple. Edit what you have to say to as short a statement as
  possible, keeping in mind that it may be difficult for the other to
  take it in. Say something like "I suspect that you don't want me to
  talk about this, but I've given it a lot of thought. I'll be brief."

- Recognize that what you're saying may be an intrusion. Particularly
  if what you have to say involves intervention, make sure you explain why you are speaking. Try "I love you and refuse to stand by
  while I see you hurting; please give me five minutes."

- If you have a history of arguing with your child, or the two of you
  tend to interrupt one another, suggest that you take turns talking.
  Ask for uninterrupted time, but make sure you offer equal time for
  a response. You could say, "I've been thinking a lot about something
  important I want to share with you. It's hard for me to express
  myself in this way, so I would appreciate your giving me five minutes of uninterrupted time to talk. Then I hope you will respond,
  and I won't interrupt you."

- Try the "brainstorming approach," where you bring up a subject,
  saying you don't have the answers but want to discuss it.

- If you're feeling judgmental, switch to an empathic point of view;
  look for your shared values rather than assuming an "I know it all"
  posture.

- Avoid mixed messages: Make sure your voice, body language, and
  expression line up with the words you're speaking.

- Respond not only to the verbal content of messages from your
  grown child but to the emotional content as well. Before discussing
  issues, acknowledge and honor the feelings being expressed, such
  as anger, sadness, or confusion.

- Check out your communication by paraphrasing what the other has said to you, to make sure you understand.

Appreciating Differences

Because your child has your genes, or may even look practically like a clone of yours, it's tempting, at some level, to assume that the two of you think and feel the same way. Unconsciously, parents often expect their children to be a copy of themselves, accepting their values and fitting into their notion of what's "normal." In fact, your child is most likely very different from yourself. There are endless variables in personality types.

"I don't know what I'm thinking until I say it out loud!" is the way one extroverted woman described her communication style. By talking, she developed her ideas, relying on the give-and-take of conversation to organize her thought process. For the first twenty-something years of her daughter's life, this mother had taken it as an affront that her daughter didn't want to engage in conversation. Eventually, she figured out that her daughter took in ideas, organized them internally, and did not speak until she had a thoroughly clear idea of what she wanted to say. Her daughter craved alone time and felt intimidated by her mother's meandering, brainstorming style of discussion.

True respect for another person involves understanding personality differences. So many communication breakdowns can be avoided when people take an objective look at how the other's mind works. If you want to make a deeper connection with an adult child, take some time to think about your different personality types.

Exercise

Use the following exercise to help you distinguish your differences from your child. Write down aspects of both of your personalities, using descriptions such as the following:

- Quiet/Talkative

- Energetic/Relaxed

- Tuned into environment/Focused inward

- Introverted/Extroverted

- Private/Outgoing

- Safety conscious/Carefree

- Learns by experimentation/Learns by following instructions

- Morning person/Night owl

- Loner/People person

- Easy-going/Critical

- Emotionally expressive/Stoic

- Accepting/Judging

Myself   **My Child**

_____   _____

_____   _____

_____   _____

_____   _____

_____   _____

_____   _____

_____   _____

_____   _____

_____   _____

_____   _____

Now, take some time to ponder your list. Think about your past interactions and ask yourself how you might proceed differently as you learn to appreciate the differences and develop more empathy for the other person's style.

Exercise

Now finish the following sentence:

When I think about the differences that exist between my child and myself, I realize that

_____

_____

_____

When I think of the similarities between us, I am aware of how

_____

_____

_____

_____

Pitfalls

When a parent reaches a new level of awareness and wants to share that new knowledge, it usually doesn't work to announce something to the effect of: "Now I see the light . . . and I'm ready to tell you all about it." Kids cringe when parents come at them with dogmatic ideas, especially if parents have credibility problems due to past lapses in caregiving. At the same time, most children, at any age, long for the love and respect of their parents. So despite what may have occurred in the past, there's usually an opening for communication. It's up to you to make the most of it. Another potential trap to avoid, as you acquire more enlightenment about the relationship, is subconsciously seeking to have your grown child give you approval or affirmation.

If you feel tempted by the short-term pleasure of getting a pat on the back from your child, you need to remember your original goal and get yourself back on track.

Keep on Keepin' On

Perhaps the most painful situation is when parents really do their part toward establishing better communication only to be rebuffed by their child. It's tempting to give up. After all the work you've done on yourself, in part for the sake of your child, it feels like a slap in the face if your child rejects your attempts to become closer. This can seem like a disaster, serving as the ultimate proof that your child is ungrateful or that you are a despicable parent. In point of fact, it may be a very positive step on the way toward mending the tie that connects you.

Whenever you make changes, especially in a profoundly important arena such as the parent-child relationship, there's bound to be some confusion and set backs. You may be a little wobbly as you take these steps, and your grown child is bound to be taken aback to a greater or lesser degree. Try to remember that confusion is healthy if it leads to positive changes in your relationship.

Rosa

Rosa made a date to take a walk on the beach with her daughter. She talked about how she was feeling, saying, among other things, "I feel uncomfortable and sad when you put me down." She also made an atonement, explaining how, as a young mother, she had imposed her own neediness on her daughter. Now she realized that the situation must have been overwhelming for a little girl. Rosa shared her feelings, "I love you, I always have and I always will. You are so special to me." Her daughter shook her head in the ocean breeze and seemed rigid. "Why are you doing this?" she asked her mom. "I want to clear things up between us," Rosa answered. "It's not that easy," her daughter said. Rosa didn't say anything more but reached over to put her arm on her daughter's shoulder. The young woman accepted the gesture and they walked together in silence.

Several things may be going on if your child does not respond to your overtures immediately:

1. Your child is testing you. Does mom really mean this? Has dad gone bonkers? Try not to be too discouraged. Your child knows that if you're really committed to making positive changes, you'll hang in there.

2. Your child wants to make a move on their own terms. You can put out an invitation for connection, but you can't be tied to a particular response. Be prepared for an overture in return, but realize it may not be exactly the response you expected.

3. It's just too soon. Your child may feel that they need to work on their problems alone, or they may not agree with you that there even is a problem. If you feel your child is putting up a hand and staying "Stop" to your attempts to communicate, find a way to be available without intruding.

4. It's overwhelming. Sometimes it's difficult for people to take in too much all at once. If you have something to communicate to your child that may prove emotional or awkward for them to hear, try to keep it simple. Let them know you're not expecting a specific response from them. Give them the time to think about it.

Consider this saying: "You can't push the river." It takes eons for the course of a river to make its way. You can't simply will it to change and see the results. But if you're patient and determined enough, eventually the riverbed will change and lead the river in a new direction. The message needs to be: I love you and I'm ready when you are.

CHAPTER 7

Mutual Love,
Individual Responsibility

*I love people. I love my family, my children . . . but inside myself is a place
where I live all alone and that's where you renew your springs that never
dry up.*

—Pearl S. Buck

*Letting others be responsible for themselves is loving and respectful.
Letting our friends and loved ones suffer the pain of growth is showing
compassion in its purest form.*

—Karen Casey, *Each Day a
New Beginning*

At birth children have no boundaries and no idea where they are in relation
to their parents or to the world. Slowly, they realize their separateness. In
their first year of life, infants go through "separation anxiety," feeling abandoned and insecure if their parents so much as leave the room.

You knew then, as you know now, that part of your job as a parent is to
help your children learn that they can survive on their own. You want them
to move from dependence to interdependence. As the years pass, you want
to see your children grow more accountable for themselves, instead of expecting unreciprocated care from others. By the time your children reach

adulthood, you expect them to be responsible for themselves and to be responsible with others. At the same time, you want to maintain close relationships with them. But that is not always how things work out. Often people's boundaries get blurred, usually due to some childhood situation where they felt intruded upon or rejected, and that can lead to problems between adult children and their parents.

On one end of the spectrum, there are the kids who can't seem to leave home, either physically or symbolically—they need too much from their parents. When parents in this situation face questions about providing shelter, money, or support, they need to learn where to draw the line between helping and becoming oppressed by grown kids. On the other end of the spectrum, there are the kids who "draw the line" far away, keeping their parents at a distance. As parents try to create a bridge, they need to discover how to encourage more closeness without crossing the line into intrusiveness.

When Grown Children Cleave to Their Parents

Today, many parents are dealing with troublesome issues with grown kids who don't seem to want to enter the adult world. Often these parents become angry, but then feel guilty because they're not able to lovingly "help" their own offspring. They don't want to be giving so much of their time, money, and energy to do something that their adult child should be handling. It's natural to feel impinged upon when a grown person intrudes on you.

You have the right to protect the inner core of your identity and to make choices that are the best for yourself. Connection with others should nourish you, and unconditional love is the highest form of connection. When love is channeled in healthy ways, both the recipient and the giver will blossom. But distortion occurs when unconditional love for someone else turns one against oneself.

It is essential to maintain your limits, to ask for what you want and need, and to nurture yourself. This builds an inner strength that can help you detect when a relationship has become intrusive or depleting. But your detector may not work so well when the person crossing the line into your personal territory is your own flesh and blood.

At times, it's tempting to abandon yourself for what you believe is the sake of your child. Lynn has intermittently given up her own activities and sense of privacy to "take care of" her son when, at forty-three, he's long overdue to take care of himself. Similarly, Richard has compromised the peacefulness of his retirement years to provide child care for his grandkids nearly every day. These parents are not helping themselves or their families by doing so much. It's not necessarily the specific act of helping but the aspect of self-sacrifice that signifies trouble. You must be whole and intact, at peace in your own life, to truly share your love with others.

Loving does not preclude being discriminating or assertive. If you find yourself denying or squelching your own needs, you may be fostering dependence rather than interdependence. Interdependence requires reciprocity. The goal is separateness and respect. If your bottom line disappears, there is a danger that one person could be lost in the process, and it could be you.

It can be sheer delight to help a grown child when you do so on your own terms. Working side by side toward a shared goal can deepen relationships while getting things done. Jake has reached a time in his life when he'd enjoy nothing more than helping his grandkids build models or do their homework, thus taking some of the pressure off his daughter. Kathryn gets personal pleasure from helping her daughter with the hors d'oeuvres for a big party. They're choosing to give of themselves because the activity is satisfying.

One man, a retired physician, talked about metaphorically "washing his son's feet," when the young man, also a doctor, returned home with a back injury after years overseas where he was working to eradicate polio in nonindustrialized countries. This father was in the throes of writing a novel, was busy with foundation work, and had his calendar filled with meetings and golf dates, but he set everything aside for two months to devote himself to his son's healing. The young man got better, returned to his work, and was later bestowed with a prestigious honor for his success in saving lives. His father said he would always treasure the memory of their time together and had the added satisfaction of knowing he had played a small part in his son's contributions to world health.

There is no checklist that will tell you, objectively, which type of assistance qualifies you as a loving supporter and which type of assistance qualifies you as a sap. It's up to you to gauge the propriety of specific decisions. But later in this chapter there are checklists for assessing whether you have a tendency toward becoming enmeshed with your child or if you have trouble setting limits. If you're paying attention, your intuition will probably tell you when it's help and when it's undermining autonomy.

When They Come Home to Live

The phenomenon of grown-up children returning to the nest has become more and more common. With today's economic fluctuations and increased longevity, it often makes sense for young people to spend more of their youthful years at home. Life at home can become a problem, though, when young people are ready for autonomy but can't seem to cope with life on their own. Some call it the "boomerang syndrome," with the unhappy implication that parents are trying to toss their kids out into the world only to have them return again and again.

Some adult kids get caught in the boomerang syndrome because they have been showered with attention and indulgence and simply don't know how to live on their own. Others haven't had enough attention, so they continue to demand it, creating a climate of hostility. Resentment makes parents feel stingier about sharing their resources, and, as a direct result, their kids may feel even more desperate and needy.

Often, the best approach for helping kids with autonomy problems is to help them establish a living arrangement with loving but firm guidelines. That doesn't necessarily mean giving over one's home, pocketbook, and life in order to support them, but it can mean giving a generous amount of sympathy, creative thought, honesty, and guidance to help grown children learn how to support themselves.

People who are at ease in the world and comfortable creating nests of their own tend to be those who have already had the experience of feeling comfortable and competent in the family home. Thus, parents can be of real help if they are prepared to look at the ways they may have failed to adequately prepare their children for the world. They can take a leadership role when they are given a new opportunity (though it may not feel like an opportunity at first) to help their adult children learn self-sufficiency while still attaining a sense of security at home. The process works best in a loving environment, and that can be a challenge when a parent is feeling resentful or intruded upon. But sympathy can grow out of an honest look at the past.

Tom

Tom was surprised by his upset reaction when his daughter wanted to move home. He'd doted on her when she was a child. Relatives had always said he'd spoiled his daughter and favored her over his two boys. Now she wanted to move home—just at the time when he and his wife were looking forward to selling the family home and traveling. She was so wrapped up in her own excitement about law school that she didn't seem to consider that her plans might conflict with her parents'.

Tom retreated into his study, buried himself in his books, and began writing in his journal again, something he hadn't done in years. Out of his writing he became aware of his longing to express through poetry the deeply creative part of himself that had been buried during the years he had worked as an English professor, writing literary criticism, and playing the academic game.

As he recognized his current needs at this phase of his life, he realized that over the years he had been so busy meeting other people's needs, including his daughter's, that he had inadvertently become overprotective at the expense of his own creativity. He had even done many of her school projects for her. But he had failed to give her the structure necessary to develop self-responsibility.

Now, he would have to find a way to help her gain the skills she needed to live on her own, without giving up his own dreams. As a compromise, he and his wife decided to go ahead and sell the house and keep their travel plans, without abandoning their daughter. Tom had an honest talk with her, and came up with a plan for her to live on her own in the condominium that was to be the parents' home base. His daughter could live there while they were traveling, and they'd be together between trips.

Tom shared with his daughter his realizations about the part he probably played in fostering her dependency, but he also helped her set up a budget and schedule, stayed in regular communication, and offered her the assurance that her parents would always love her.

Tom's circumstances allowed for a compromise that suited both him and his daughter. In most situations where a grown child moves home, however, the parents don't have the option of leaving. Usually, the issue is whether the grown child will move in with the parents, and share the home once again. Some parents simply say "no"—especially if there's been a history of inappropriate expectations on the part of the grown kid that parents will "take care of" him or her. Only the individual parent can determine whether saying "no" is necessary.

In many cases, however, it can work to have a dependent child return "one more time"—if, this time, the parent has a clear idea of the mutual goals and is willing to invest time, creativity, and energy toward making this homecoming the one that will prepare the adult child for a successful flight from the nest.

Attention to the relationship is crucial. It doesn't work in most families to resume the old parent-child roles. Becoming a caregiver can be draining for the parent and undermine the child's motivation for leaving home. Having clear expectations that everyone in the household will contribute what they can to chores, finances, and family life is also essential.

Still, it helps to admit that everyone is losing some autonomy in the situation—not just the kids but also the parents, as Patricia Schiff Estess explained in her article the November 1994 issue of *Modern Maturity.*

"All this unexpected togetherness leaves both sides with mixed emotions. The kids, while grateful (we choose to believe) to have a safe and comfortable haven in which to await opportunity's knock, also resent their own lack of privacy, economic independence and control. . . . Yes, they can share in the chores, watch the house when we're away, and they can be great company. Yet we too lose our autonomy, our privacy, our space, and our hair dryers. We fall into familiar parenting traps: nagging them to clean their rooms, waiting for them to come in at night, bugging them to be more aggressive in their job search."

For grown children to get much-needed practice in becoming competent, contributing members of a household, they need to be treated as full-fledged adults. They deserve respect for their way of doing things, and parents deserve the same. Still, this is not a "roommate" situation, where people lead separate lives, trying to stay out of each other's way. Pretending to be disconnected individuals simply sharing a home precludes the greater possibilities for growth—for parents and grown kids— that can come from clarifying relationships and enjoying the benefits of family life.

The following suggestions offer some ways to maximize the potential for a win/win situation when a grown kid moves back home:

- Make a written list of agreements.

- Delineate chores and make clear when they should be done.

- Decide what kind of "tabs" you'll keep on one another. (Do you let each other know when you'll be home?)

- Make plans for certain shared activities, whether that means dinner together certain days or a weekly outing or other activities that will bring you together as a family.

- Establish a regular time for "clearing the air," when everyone in the household gets together to discuss what's working and what's not working, so together you can work out a plan to make the arrangement more comfortable for everyone.

- Discuss privacy issues, including signals you can give to one another when you want some alone time.

- Allow for separate use of the house, or certain parts of the house, on certain occasions, including when someone wants to entertain guests. (One option to consider is asking for the house for yourself at certain times and, if you're generous, allowing your child to have the house for entertaining.)

- Have a set time for bill paying so everyone knows what the expenses are and each makes appropriate contributions.

- Discuss common courtesies, and emphasize the need to treat one another politely throughout the day.

- If your grown child needs to accomplish something—such as finding a job, finishing school, or dealing with an addiction—make it known that you expect to see progress: maybe meeting weekly to discuss the employment search, meeting with a grown child's therapist or AA sponsor, or looking over college grades together. This should not become a "control" issue—nor an opportunity for parents to nag or for adult children to make excuses—but rather a method of mutual support. You get the satisfaction of seeing progress; your child gets the benefit of your involvement.

The immediate goal is to make life together happy and smooth. The long-term goal is for the grown child to feel comfortable and competent and thereby more confident about the prospects for leaving the nest.

Instead of the "boomerang syndrome," writer Bo Niles prefers the term "home again" syndrome. In the August 1996 issue of *Country Living*, Niles explains her college-educated grown son moved home to save money while launching his film career. She realized this was normal enough, having recently read the statistic that 32 percent of adult males between the ages of twenty-five and thirty-four still lived at home. And she was very fond of her son. Her family had to develop what she called "a new rhythm," which worked out fine.

"Community. Commune. Communicate. These are the principles that guide us, as they do—or should—any congenial group, be it an office or a town meeting or a picnic. And, so far it is working out just fine. When David finally spreads his wings and flies away from us and our nest, I know we will miss this phase of our life with him very much. It's been fun having him around," Niles wrote.

Niles's family happily adapted to a grown child moving home. But when relationships are less comfortable, parents must pay close attention to the family's dynamics. Often, kids misdirect their needs for independence by placing demands on their parents rather than placing demands on themselves. At times like these, parents need to get some emotional distance to define their own boundaries while at the same time preserving their feelings of love for their child.

Tom

Tom realized he had to let his daughter know that he wasn't going to encourage her dependence on her family. Although he would provide her with love and support, those came with clear expectations about her part of the agreement for her house-sitting in the family home while her parents traveled. She was to pay the bills. Her parents also arranged for a mentor—a family friend—to meet regularly with her as she worked to establish herself in a career.

When you say to your kids "things are going to change," you want to say that from a place of calmness, not from a place of confrontation. It's likely that you and your grown child share the same goal. The message is: Now you are an adult, I expect you to behave as an adult. Adults can experience joy from feeling competent and accomplished. It's a gift to your kids to help them, but only if you can let go of your own anger, be clear about your own needs, and offer your hand in love.

When They Make Bad Choices and Cry "Help"

The boomerang syndrome can be dangerous for parents who are constantly waiting for the next blow to come from children who seem bent on self-destruction and wreak havoc in the lives of those who care for them. In these situations, parents might legitimately ask themselves if they are contributing to their grown child's problems by providing a safety net that's always available when the child falls. In the worst cases, parents decide to "divorce" their children. There are some situations where parents actually go into hiding and move away with no forwarding address, so that a troublesome child can't find them. Often, this happens after a history of abusive behavior on the part of the disturbed child.

Again, this decision is one that can be made only by the individual —there are no hard and fast rules for deciding whether it's "too late" to help a grown child and if the only option is to save one's own sanity—but severing all ties is the nuclear weapon of family relationships. Instead of cutting ties, parents may decide instead to look deep within themselves for the love it takes to be truly creative. Sometimes when parents go through a careful self-analysis and recognize their contributions to their children's troubles, they can develop a new empathy that enables them to establish a healing bond with a child. Often, this self-analysis can't be done alone; but there are many places to seek assistance.

Lynn

When Lynn started attending Al-Anon meetings, she expected she would talk about her problem with her son. Instead she ended up talking about herself. Lynn had been taught to be a good girl. She was trained from an early age to focus on the moral obligation to care for others first. Her focus was always outward. She did not value her inner self. She was socialized to be ladylike, which in her family meant never to show anger, and always to remain calm, kind, and superpatient. She was not to ask for the nurturing she needed, and she centered her life around pleasing her parents. Lynn grew up to be a very self-effacing person, habitually putting aside her own needs and desires for those of others. She'd never learned to define her own physical or psychological "space." In her Al-Anon meetings, she learned that she had become a martyr to her desire to please and take care of others.

Now, feeling suffocated by her needy grown son, she needed to set some limits with him, for his sake as well as hers. Before, she had been propelled by guilt and an overdeveloped sense of responsibility to do things for her son. Now, with her new understanding of her own needs she expected something in return. She didn't want to play the martyr role any longer.

For people who grew up in families that violated their sense of self-worth, it's a challenge to teach their own kids to respect themselves and others. But when these parents end up, in turn, with grown children who run all over them, expect the world, and never do their part in life, they suddenly have to do a quick study, learning as much as they can about setting limits before their kids take over their lives. Obviously it's difficult to undo your own conditioning and habits—or inspire your children to do so—all at once. But you can start by clarifying the past, making a plan for the future, and getting support.

Lynn

It wasn't until the day she came home and felt ill at the sight of her son's truck that Lynn was forced to confront her own problems with boundaries. She came to see how she had "babied" her son because of his difficult life experiences—losing his father, getting into fights at school, going to war—that she had not been able to prevent. She realized that, now, she needed to delineate her appropriate role in the situation. She shared with him her new awareness about the destructive nature of their past interactions. She talked about her love for him and her confidence in his ability to do the right thing—stay in treatment, keep his job, and pay his way at home with the goal of establishing his own life. With this understanding, she was able to embark on a "one more time" plan for having him live at home under mutually agreed-upon terms.

Money

Money is both symbolic and of real import between parents and grown children. Everything from who picks up the tab for dinner out, to the price of gifts, to inheritance plans and loans for major purchases can become significant issues in the relationship. In unhealthy relationships, money can be used intentionally to exert control, reward obedience, placate or belittle someone, send hidden messages, or stir up sibling rivalry. Money tends to carry less symbolism among companionable adults; but even in healthy relationships, problems can develop if financial issues are left undiscussed. Attention to the issue of money can lessen its power over people.

It's as ridiculous to pretend that "money is nothing" as it is to act as though "money is everything." Betty Frain's brother, Jim Frain, a marketing executive, has observed over the years that people who start business relationships with the attitude that "money is no object" often are the very ones to turn around later and emotionally overreact to money issues. In families, just as in business, the significance of monetary exchange must be recognized and discussed.

It's emotionally liberating for families to be able to discuss their financial needs, interdependence, and plans for handling estates after death. Parents can set an example by putting the money issues out in a nonthreatening way and opening the door to discussion. For families who do not have a history of handling money openly or wisely, seeking expertise is valuable. A consultation with a financial planner, or a book on financial agreements, can be useful. However you choose to approach these issues, you should proceed with the awareness that money carries different symbolic meanings to different people.

Many issues between parents and their adult children are based on a healthy give-and-take attitude. You want to be generous, but you want to take care of yourself. Knowing your limits—and communicating them—allows for the happy, rather than begrudging, sharing of your resources, including your money and your time.

Lending money can be of great benefit to the parent–adult child relationship, as long as it doesn't compromise the parent's budget or undermine the grown child's need to develop personal responsibility.

Michael

Michael was glad to loan his son and daughter-in-law the down payment on a house, knowing that it would help them start building equity instead of throwing their money away on rent. But when his son dropped some hints about wanting to buy a new car that was beyond his budget, Michael tactfully made it clear that he wouldn't help with that purchase. Watching his son grow more free with his credit card usage, Michael became concerned about his son's tendency toward extravagance. He decided it would be meddling to lecture about money management. But when his son brought up the subject, Michael made a lighthearted comment about differentiating between the "need-it" and "want-it" categories of things.

How much *time* to devote to your grown children and grandchildren is an individual choice that comes, ideally, from a conscious assessment of your resources, needs, and desires. As with money, issues about time can have both symbolic and real importance.

Grandparents: The Right Kind of Closeness

What a joy: this opportunity to be close to a child when you have the benefits of more time, experience, knowledge, and understanding of children than you probably had when your kids were young. Loving grandparents treasure their time with grandchildren and look for ways to stay connected. Some, like Jake and Don, are willing to go to great lengths—crossing geographic and emotionally difficult boundaries—to get closer to their grandchildren. For them, the challenge is to create a place for themselves in their grandchildren's lives, by making overtures that demonstrate the important role they can play as grandparents.

Don

In a telephone conversation with his daughter, Don acknowledged that he didn't recall too much about babies since he had been an old-fashioned father who wasn't as hands-on as he might have been. He expressed his genuine curiosity about what gifts his new grandson might enjoy having. His daughter talked to him about the latest theories on educational baby toys, and Don used his wood-working skills to create an infant play structure with bright objects that hung within the baby's reach. The overture expressed not only his willingness to devote time to the baby, but his eagerness to learn his daughter's preferences and respond to them—a departure from his past tendencies to bestow attention and gifts on his terms.

Jake

Jake wrote a letter to his grandchildren telling them about his recent ride on an old, renovated steam train. He enclosed photographs of the train and explained that, when he was a boy, trains were a common form of transportation. "What's your favorite kind of transportation?" he asked the grandchildren in the letter. That began a back-and-forth correspondence that gave him an opportunity to send them stories, articles, and pictures about their favorite vehicles—which turned out to be airplanes and mountain bikes. By learning more about the children's likes and dislikes, he was able to demonstrate his interest in them as individuals. The exchange provided inspiration for activities when they got together, such as visiting airplane museums, renting mountain bikes, and going to bike races.

Others, like Richard, have frequent contact with grandkids but need to set limits so that their time together continues to be valued by both grandparents and grandchildren. If grandparents are fulfilled in their own lives, they have more to offer, and that can't happen if they're at the beck and call of their kids needing child care.

Richard

Richard's wife noticed that he was neglecting his own recreation, fishing and golf, just as she was playing less tennis and having fewer hours to herself for her artwork. On the day when the grandkids complained about having to sit in front of the television—and Richard seemed uncharacteristically annoyed—his wife decided to say something to him.

As they began talking, Richard realized that he had confused being loving and available to his grandkids with sacrificing all of his recreational time for them. As a result, his time with them had become less joyful and more routine. He felt depleted and empty after spending time with them. He wanted to laugh and have a good time with them but didn't really feel like it. Finally, he decided to discuss the problem with his minister. During the conversation he realized that he was unhappy but was controlling his unhappiness because of the guilt he felt about not being much of a family man when his own kids were growing up.

Ultimately, he was able to admit to himself that, although he wanted to continue spending time with his grandkids, those visits had to be more on his terms. It seemed like a risk to talk with his son and daughter-in-law about their last-minute requests for babysitting, but he could no longer allow his own life to remain off balance. He also realized it would be good for his son's family to have another source of child care. After all, the kids would be going to school one day, and they needed to socialize with other children. Once he looked at the situation objectively, he was then able to consider ways to approach his son without guilt about the past or fear of future rejection.

Many people hope for simple consideration from their children and may expect that their kids will "get the hint" on their own. An essential part of maintaining healthy relationships is clear communication. You can't expect others to read your mind, and you may be sending signals that are the opposite of how you feel.

Richard's son may not have known that his parents had other activities that were being set aside each time they had the grandchildren over, even though Richard had been growing more and more annoyed. Often the only way people can communicate is to get mad first. But loving parents try to do their own work so they can avoid becoming embroiled in the counterproductive conflicts that can threaten the quality of relationships.

When your kids seem to be asking too much of you, ask yourself, "Would a friend ask this?" If the answer is "no," then it's time for change. There are, of course, an increasing number of families in which grandparents become primary caregivers out of necessity, because their children are incapable of doing so themselves. There may seem to be no other choice.

When grandparents choose to become parents to young children again they may enjoy the satisfaction of making a Herculean contribution to the health of their family. Others may decide it's best to step in temporarily while a more appropriate long-term solution is found. Parents who have become solely responsible for grandchildren can greatly benefit from books on this specialized subject and support groups that are available. See "Organizations That Can Help" and "References and Resources" at the end of this book for support groups and books for grandparents.

Regardless of the logistics of the relationship between grandparents and grandchildren—whether you live under the same roof or 3,000 miles apart—you can have a tremendously positive influence, particularly if you have a good memory of your own parenting years. Chances are, your child's parenting techniques include many of the same strengths and weaknesses that you demonstrated as a parent. Although it's often unwise to meddle in your child's parenting, you are in a unique position to recognize and respond to your grandchildren's emotional needs, as well as to give them the most valuable gift of all—relaxed time together.

At this point, it may be helpful to look at problems you have with limit-setting that may have preceded the birth of your own children and contributed to issues you may be facing today. By doing the following exercise, you may be able to see how your own conditioning contributed to the problem. Then you can have more sympathy and love for your grown child.

Checklist: Do You Have Problems Setting Limits?

Answer "yes" or "no" to the following questions:

_____ Do you do things for others that they can do for themselves?

_____ Do you protect others' feelings at the expense of your own?

_____ Do you have a hard time saying "no" and sticking to it?

_____ Do you try to immediately "fix it" if someone is upset?

_____ Do you fail to ask for what you need and settle for what you get?

_____ Do you rescue people from their irresponsible behavior?

_____ Do you lie for others to cover for their mistakes or irresponsible acts?

_____ Do you allow others to make even mundane choices for you?

_____ Do you take on more than your fair share of the work or responsibility?

_____ Do you frequently stay in the company of people who leave you feeling depleted or blue?

_____ Do you often appreciate others' potential so much that you tend to overlook their present poor behavior?

_____ Are you fooled by some small improvement here or there rather than looking at the larger picture?

_____ Do you see poor behaviors as isolated acts, rather than as part of a larger pattern?

Obviously, all of us do some of these things sometimes, but if you do many of them frequently then the chances are that you grew up without a clear sense of where you end and others begin. Once you understand that you have trouble setting limits, you can embark on a conscious effort to be a person who cares for yourself, as well as for others. This can have a liberating effect in all of your relationships, not just with your grown children but also with your co-workers, friends, and other family members. At first, people might be put off by the change in you, especially if it means you won't "drop everything" for their needs as you may have done in the past. But ultimately, your relationships will be more satisfying.

Checklist: Is Your Grown Child's Life Merging with Yours?

Answer "yes" or "no" to the following questions:

_____ Are thoughts about your child your main worry and concern?

_____ Do you feel repeatedly hurt by your grown child?

_____ Do you feel confused by your loyalty or commitment to your child?

_____ Do you feel you're giving without reciprocity?

_____ Are you wanting to say "no" but having trouble doing so?

_____ Are you so accustomed to excuses and alibis that you are satisfied with minimal improvement or partial promise keeping by your child?

_____ Do you fear a loss of your privacy, money, or property?

_____ Do you feel your peace and quiet shattered by the behavior of a grown child?

_____ Does your child put you down?

If you answered "yes" to any of the above questions, it wouldn't hurt to examine your own issues. If you answered "yes" to several questions, you'll need to take some action to avoid the takeover of your life by your child or to prevent a blow-up that may result in wanting to "divorce" your child. It's okay to feel angry; that can be the impetus for making changes. But you'll be more effective if you can realize that the problem is probably not caused just by your "bad kid," but, in part, by the whole family system.

Often, the problem with the "tough love" solution to dilemmas is that parents are so angry they emphasize the "tough" rather than the "love." You can avoid this by developing empathy, which can help you get back to a place of love. From a loving place, you can be objective and strong and still show your grown child that your setting of limits is not a punishment, power play, or withdrawal of affection. Rather, setting clear limits frees both of you to explore your own lives. Parents often need support for setting limits with grown kids and need help to stick with their plan. You can turn to church groups, women's or men's groups, psychotherapy, twelve-step programs, and sometimes friends to help you remain objective and clear in your goals.

You may be overly sensitive to the needs of others, sometimes at the expense of your own. If you have these tendencies and are dealing with an intrusive grown child, you probably need to handle some of your own issues before you can discuss your concerns with your child. You need a clear plan, in writing, that defines what you expect from your grown child in return for the gifts of your time, money, or energy. You'll define a reciprocity that takes your needs into account with equal weight given to your grown child's needs.

Exercise

Try the following exercise to help you define your needs and those of your grown child, for the moment setting aside the concern about what happens when the two are in conflict.

My needs are:

_____

_____

_____

_____

_____

My grown child's needs are:

_____

_____

_____

_____

_____

What I can do to meet my grown child's needs without compromising my own:

_____

_____

_____

_____

_____

Lynn

Here's how Lynn's list looked:

My needs are to have:

- *Knowledge that my son is working toward establishing his own home*

- *Privacy, peace and quiet, and my choice of music*

- *Freedom from fear of verbal abuse or implied physical threat from my son*

- *Financial stability (not to be financially drained by my son)*

- *Time to myself*

- *Fun without always worrying about him*

- *My property respected*

- *A clean house*

- *Knowledge that he's committed to his alcohol treatment*

My son's needs are to have:

- *Alcohol treatment*

- *A place to live*

- *A job/income*

- *Friends*

- *A feeling of being loved*

- *Problem-solving skills*

- *The ability to give and take*

- *The ability to grieve (especially over his father's death)*

What I'm willing to do:

- *Pay for drug treatment, on the condition that he follows through*

- *Let him stay at my home for six months with house rules (he does some chores, respects my privacy in certain rooms, and treats me respectfully) on the condition he gets a job and pays rent*

- *Spend time with my son during which I talk about our past and show him my love*

- *Tell my son what my needs are*

- *Share my own grief over his father's death*

- *Offer to help him set up his own household as soon as possible*

Once you have your list, you can define your boundaries more clearly, asking yourself: "Are my child's needs impinging too much on my own?" You'll also be in a position to describe your needs articulately and explain what you're willing and able to do for your child. This can come from a loving place. Most people respond to honesty and clarity. Use the suggestions from the preceding chapter on communication. Whether or not you end up with the satisfaction of seeing your child grow into a productive adult, by doing the work necessary to be loving and by clearly delineating your expectations, you can attain a sense of peace by knowing you have done all you can.

When Grown Kids Become Alienated

Being too involved with a grown child's problems is one manifestation of problems with autonomy. The opposite also occurs. Sometimes grown children push parents away, ostensibly as a way to achieve a sense of self. In these situations, it helps to keep in mind what we know about adult development and family systems: the possibility that temporarily alienated children may be going through a healthy separation process. But when the separation is hostile, goes on too long, or looks as though it may be permanent, then it's likely that the distance is causing suffering for the grown child as well as for the parent.

Sometimes kids reject parents completely. Usually, they are stuck in a state of blame that can prevent their own healthy development and prevent them from getting the emotional satisfaction that comes from involvement with a healthy extended family. Parents who have been rejected may feel helpless when they're being kept away from their child and communication seems impossible.

When an adult child refuses contact, the best you can do is communicate clearly that you'll be available whenever your child is ready. And you can use the time to explore the factors that may have contributed to the alienation. Parents in this situation—just like parents whose kids are intruding—may feel angry but must get past their anger before they can hope for change. Self-examination and evaluation of your relationship—using the exercises presented earlier in this book—deepen understanding and lead to the kind of real empathy that can move emotional mountains.

Rosa

Rosa knew she had to take a fresh approach to the relationship with her daughter. The hostility crackling between them was the flip side to the powerful pull between them since her daughter's childhood.

For so many years, Rosa had devoted herself to helping her daughter out, including those horrific teenage years when her daughter sometimes would stay out all night and would take all kinds of risks, including experimentation with drugs. Rosa had become so absorbed with worry that her daughter's life had become more important to Rosa than her own. As a single mom, Rosa felt that she had to give up her opportunities for fun to take care of her daughter. She sacrificed promotions, broke up with boyfriends, and assumed her daughter's burdens as her own.

She'd cover for her daughter, calling the school and making excuses, let her daughter stay home sick, and hover over her. Her daughter felt smothered. At the same time, Rosa was subconsciously feeling smothered herself. When her daughter moved out at age eighteen, she'd sometimes call and wake Rosa up in the middle of the night, making Rosa's boyfriend furious. She seemed to know that her mother would drop everything for her, at any time. Rosa and her daughter had developed a co-dependent relationship. Through the years, they had been overly enmeshed in one another's lives. Rosa felt too responsible for her daughter and neglected her own needs. Her daughter wound up feeling controlled, devalued, incompetent, and very, very angry. They would fight, but then Rosa's daughter would feel guilty for "all her mother had done" and would behave in a "good little girl" way, seeking her mother's approval.

With the boundary between their two lives so blurred, Rosa and her daughter did not go through the gradual process of separation that's healthy for growing children. Her daughter needed to claim her own autonomy but was unable to do so until she was out of the house and got her own life together. When the break came, it was a dramatic one.

Once she felt secure in her own life, she felt the need to reject her mother in order to demonstrate her independence. She would refuse to return her mother's phone calls for weeks at a time, and went months without visiting—even though she lived in the same town. After a hiatus of contact, she would show up for a visit at her mother's house but usually would make some rude remark.

After the brunch when Rosa felt humiliated by her daughter's put-down, Rosa talked to a counselor. She realized she could not stand for such treatment. After a few counseling sessions, Rosa began to understand the dynamic at work—her daughter wanted to feel free of the sense of obligation toward her mother. Rosa faced the difficult reality of the situation: It had taken years to create the unhealthy relationship with her daughter, and it might take years to make it better.

The day she talked with her daughter on the beach, acknowledging the mistakes she had made as a parent, was a small step. Rosa realized she would have to wait awhile before taking the next step. In order to have a "clean slate," Rosa would have to assure her daughter that there were no leftover "debts." Rosa demonstrated her dedication to a fresh start by giving her daughter time to think about the conversation, rather than pushing for closure. Until trust developed between them, Rosa contented herself with the knowledge that her daughter was doing fine in her own life.

It still hurts, but once parents get an idea about what has caused their child to become alienated, at least they can try to find a way to share what they have learned. In Rosa's case, it would mean looking for an opening to connect in a positive way. But that would take time.

Sometimes alienation is only a temporary situation. Often it's not particularly hostile, it's just uncomfortable. At times like this, you need to realize there's an ebb and flow in relationships: What's appropriate now may not be appropriate at another time. But we can try to influence the situation in a way that we believe will help everyone.

Jake

Jake's breakthrough in communication with his daughter followed his realizations about the past. Once he confronted his mistakes as a parent—including how he had intruded on his daughter's privacy but had failed to show up for important events—he could understand her current reluctance to welcome him into her life.

Instead of feeling insulted that his daughter was rebuffing his plans to move to her town, Jake found ways to see the logic in her response. Jake had been inaccessible to and inconsiderate of his daughter years ago. It followed that she would be suspicious of his overtures now. She justifiably feared he would make unreasonable demands on her attention, which is already spread thin, now that she is in the middle of her child-rearing years and a burgeoning career. It was only after Jake went deeper—setting aside the surface messages to look for their causes—that he was able to have the kind of genuine communication with her that offered hope for the future.

When you seek to change your relationship as a result of your own personal growth, it's important to be aware whether you're sending out confusing signals to your children. Remember how you were when your children were growing up, and realize that's how they expect you to be now. It's part of the dynamics of family relationships to move closer or further apart, but it can be perplexing if the moves are not explained. Communication creates the bridge.

Beth

Beth realized she had a long way to go before she could be open about her feelings with her son. She wanted to spend more time with him but could not come up with the right words to express that sentiment in a graceful way. After all, she'd spent her life up to this point being reserved. But she decided to start with a small overture. During a telephone conversation with her son, she sympathized with his busy schedule and his concerns about spending holidays with his in-laws. He and his wife probably would welcome time for themselves along with their visits to family. "You know, it doesn't have to be a formal holiday for you to drive up. How about the two of you coming here for a weekend getaway? We'll just relax and have fun. I always love having you stay here, but if you want more privacy, there's a new bed-and-breakfast nearby. If you can make the time, I'll make the arrangements."

It's not being "needy" to wish for closeness, just as it's not "meddling" for a parent to want to continue nurturing. The goal is to connect without becoming enmeshed. In her book *Breaking Free of the Shame Trap* (1994), psychologist Christine Brautigam Evans says that autonomy involves finding the fine line:

"I prefer to think of autonomy as the capacity to act on behalf of our own best interests, with a compassionate consideration of the effect our actions have on those around us but without letting their needs dictate our choices."

Wouldn't it be ideal to be able to share your time and affection with your kids without ever having to worry that the relationship might take over your life or suddenly be taken away? These fears of co-dependence or abandonment thrive in silence but evaporate when needs are expressed in a loving way that is not overbearing to either party. You can take the lead in opening communication. You don't need to say the words "boundaries," "limits," or "closeness," but you can find the words and actions that will help you share your insights with your children. Your love, self-understanding, and communication skills will help you find solutions to the ongoing dilemma of how to draw a line between yourself and others, without abandonment or enmeshment. You can celebrate your individuality while creating a welcoming space where you know you and your loved ones belong together.

CHAPTER 8

Uninvited Intervention

Making the decision to have a child—it's momentous. It is to decide forever to have your heart go walking around outside your body.

—Elizabeth Stone

Pain and suffering may often seem to be calling us to jump in and fix things, but perhaps they are asking us first to be still enough to hear what can really help, what can truly get to the cause of this suffering, what will not only eliminate it but prevent it from returning. So before we act, we need to listen.

—Mirabai Bush, *Compassion in Action*

In Greek mythology, Demeter, the Goddess of Agriculture, learns that her daughter Persephone has been kidnapped by Hades, King of the Underworld. She goes into mourning, refusing to allow anything to grow. Winter reigns, threatening to kill Earth and everything on it, until Zeus, King of the Gods, intervenes to allow Demeter's rescue of her daughter. Demeter succeeds, but only part way. Because Persephone eats six forbidden pomegranate seeds on her way out of Hades' kingdom, she must stay in the Underworld for half of every year for eternity. That is why everything on Earth dies in the fall, according to the myth, because Demeter is in mourning until springtime, when her daughter emerges into the sunlight and the plants may grow again.

This myth may be disturbing, but parents experiencing the terrifying problem of a child in danger may find Demeter's problem enviable: There was no ambiguity for Demeter about whether or not to meddle. Persephone needed help and Demeter had the power to provide it. Demeter wasn't embarrassed to express grief over her grown daughter's plight; in fact, she let the whole world know she was furious and in mourning, in no uncertain terms. And no one was shedding tears over the son-in-law from Hell.

For mortals, problems aren't so clear-cut, and your power to tackle them is limited. Sometimes it's hard to tell right from wrong. Even if you can make that determination, there's confusion about what you should do when your child is in trouble. And that's on top of the social taboo that makes you feel guilty about discussing problems with kids who are "old enough to take care of themselves."

This society has encouraged parents to keep to themselves, mind their own business, and regard family privacy as primary. Historically, the desire not to get involved permitted child abuse and domestic violence to flourish. Many family problems were hidden away and kept secret. Today, thankfully, due to greater awareness about these issues, family and friends can sometimes step in to provide help and encouragement and to help break unhealthy cycles.

In the areas of domestic violence—addiction, mental illness, child development, disabilities, chronic illness, and death and dying—people are coming forward to share information rather than turning away in fear or ignorance. People are becoming more knowledgeable about psychological issues affecting their relationships. The more you know about the nature of your grown child's problem, the more effective the action you can take in becoming part of their support system. When grown children have serious problems, they may not think they need help or may ask that their problem be kept secret, which only further isolates and burdens them. Some children make excuses or lean on their parents to "help" them, while failing to do what's necessary to help themselves.

Ready for Action

Parents who are facing an immediate crisis with a grown child may have skipped ahead to this chapter, understandably. If you're worried about the health or well-being of your child, you're probably ready for action. There's no more painful circumstance for parents than seeing their children in danger.

You just want to do the right thing. It was so much easier when your kids were small. If a toddler runs out into the roadway, a parent's reaction is instinctive and instantaneous. Of course, the parent grabs the kid and pulls them to safety. The episode may cause a temporary adrenaline overdose and subsequent nightmares about what might have happened, but it's over fast, has a happy ending, and leaves no lingering questions about whether the decision to intervene was correct.

The word "intervene" means, literally, "to come between two things." This is what a parent naturally does when the two things are a toddler and an oncoming car. But, twenty years later, parents are likely to face more difficult decisions about what role to play if they see their adult children plunging headlong into dangerous situations.

What do you do when you recognize a threat to your children that they do not actively try to escape, such as an abusive partner, dependence on drugs or alcohol, or a dead-end career choice? Now you're seeing a different definition of the word "intervene"—the one that applies when one nation decides to get involved in the affairs of another country. It is a political decision. Your adult child is no longer technically part of your domestic situation. Suddenly, you're dealing with a foreign policy matter. You do not have legal responsibility for the well-being of your child, and even if you feel morally and emotionally responsible, you do not have the legal right to intervene.

If your child asks for your help, that's one thing. But what's to be done when adult children are not asking for help or are specifically asking parents to stay out of their affairs? For concerned parents, merely standing by and watching can be excruciating. The first thing you need to decide is if intervention is appropriate. The well-being of your children and grandchildren may be at stake. Knowing how to offer assistance or feedback can be tricky.

If you've gone through this book and done the exercises so far, you've already taken steps toward deepening your relationship with your grown child. You've assessed the problem with objectivity, taken inventory of your own contributions to the problem, looked deep within yourself for the reservoir of love you have for your grown child, and made an assessment of the relationship. At this point, you should have gotten some of your own emotional "baggage" out of the way, as well as minimized peripheral influences such as decorum and social pressure. You've created a solid foundation for taking action.

However, if you have skipped ahead to this chapter because of an immediate crisis and it's necessary to intervene in your grown child's problem at once, you will be wise to find some immediate support for yourself as you step in to support your child. You might go back to the beginning of this book and do the exercises while simultaneously taking action to help your child.

Use the following checklist to decide the magnitude of the problem and whether or not you should intervene immediately.

Checklist: Should You Intervene?

Immediate intervention is probably necessary if your grown child's problem seems life threatening, including if your child appears to be:

_____ Suicidal (talking about death; giving things away; saying that life is unbearable; saying that things are hopeless; possessing guns, drugs, or other implements of death; discussing plans for suicide)

_____ Depressed (crying; not eating, sleeping, or dressing; neglecting normal activities; behaving lethargically; speaking in monotone; being uncommunicative)

_____ Homicidal (talking about killing or hurting someone else)

_____ A victim of violence (having unexplained injuries, bruises, or broken bones; making implausible excuses for injuries; behaving as if they are fearful; lacking privacy or freedom from mate)

_____ A perpetrator of violence or neglect (appears to be mistreating or ignoring the survival needs of a spouse or child)

_____ Participating in dangerous drug or alcohol abuse or the sale of drugs (drives under the influence, cares for children while drunk or stoned, becomes irresponsible or dangerous at work due to substance abuse, acts in a way that suggests drug dealing)

Consider intervening under circumstances where your grown child is struggling with an overwhelming life condition, such as:

_____ Chronic illness or complicated recovery from surgery

_____ Reaction to a trauma, such as being raped, robbed, or injured in an accident; or grief at the death of a loved one

_____ Job loss, career change, or a difficult move

_____ Child-rearing or parenting problem

_____ Divorce

_____ Relationship/marriage dysfunction

_____ Phobia or panic disorder

_____ Eating disorder

_____ Addiction to gambling

_____ Obsession with sexual activity

_____ Financial crisis such as credit card abuse or bankruptcy

Life-Threatening Problems

If your grown child has a problem in the life-threatening category, remember that you can only do so much. The goal of intervention is not a complete cure nor an amelioration of pain, but the offering of an ally and an additional support system to your child during a time of extreme turmoil or crisis.

You can't solve your child's problems, as much as you'd like to. You can only hope to facilitate a healing process. To protect your own boundaries in the process, it helps to set a limit at the very beginning on the amount of time and energy you are willing to give. It's also imperative that you help your child build bridges to other supports. Attempting to carry all the responsibility yourself will likely only create more anxiety for everyone.

Community resources and the help of other family members will be essential. Pick up the phone. Find the hot lines, hospitals, law enforcement officials, shelters, clergy, support groups, physicians, and others with expertise in the problem. Don't be shy about talking to friends. Real friends will stand by you and offer their help in expanding your support network and in finding the best resources.

Don't minimize your role. Sometimes families fail to respond to emergencies for fear of creating dependence, seeming intrusive, or undermining a person's independence. Although you can't fix your child's problem, your help can be profound. Many adult children wish their parents would notice their pain and ask how they can be of help. Too often, parents lose the opportunity to provide support because they fear involvement.

It's best when parents refrain from the temptation to criticize, dwell on, or judge their children's mistakes and faults. It helps to remember your own human failings, shortcomings, and youthful naivete.

Domestic Violence

Violence in the home can take many forms. There are the extreme cases of repeated physical attacks or sexual abuse of a spouse or child, and more subtle forms of abuse, including verbal intimidation, put-downs, and the creation of an atmosphere of fear. Generally, the victim loses all self-respect and becomes increasingly powerless, thus allowing the cycle to continue and worsen. Usually, the abuser manipulates the victim into believing that he or she deserves the abusive treatment and is not able to function outside of the relationship. The insidious emotional power that the abuser wields over the victim often creates a difficult challenge for anyone trying to intervene.

Mark
Mark is losing sleep and weight because of his worries about the safety of his daughter and grandson. Once he began to suspect his son-in-law was being abusive, Mark began to see more and more signs of

their mistreatment. His gut is telling him to march over to their house and confront his son-in-law, but his daughter still talks as if nothing is wrong.

If you confront grown children about bruises, their uncharacteristic failure to attend family functions, or other signs of possible abuse, usually their first response will be denial, regardless of the truth. In the case of Mark's daughter, as with many people dealing with violence at home, all the indicators are there: Her husband is from an abusive family, he is heavy drinker, and he's excessively possessive of Mark's daughter and grandson. Sometimes parents need to trust their own observations and not what they're told, as the situation could preclude an honest response from their child.

Loving parents will not give up if they believe a grown child is in an abusive situation or if they suspect grandchildren are being mistreated. They will continue reaching out. You can't force your children to leave their situations, but you can do research so that you know who will be available to help them when they are ready.

In situations of domestic violence, statistics show that unless victims of abuse get good therapy, they will continue going back to their abusers or find someone else who treats them the same way. It's a cycle that repeats over and over again unless someone intervenes.

It's okay to repeat the message that you're aware of a problem. Let it be known you see something is amiss; for example, you notice that your child hasn't gone out of their house for an unusually long time or that your grandchild seems withdrawn. Invite your child to your house or out to lunch. Ask about their life. Offer yourself for child care, housecleaning, or other practical help. There is no "right" time to bring up your concerns about the possibility of abuse, but you can look for ways. Think about domestic violence just as you would an illness. Look for opportunities to show your concern, clip pertinent articles, and make occasions to get together. Don't let the subject disappear underground.

As discussed previously in this book, it's imperative to look at the influence of your family system in the present crisis. Do you recognize the part that your family may have played a role, even unwittingly, in steering someone toward an abusive situation? If so, be prepared to share your knowledge. Support and illumination may help a victim get out of the cycle. Remember too that although you can't force an adult victim to get help, you can call civil authorities if you are certain that a grandchild or another minor is being abused.

Mark

After careful consideration of the situation and calling a child abuse information line, Mark was still concerned enough to speak with his daughter about his grandson. He knew he was risking their relationship, but he decided to gamble. When she insisted all was fine, Mark warned his daughter that he was going to report his grandson's bruises to Child Protective Services. The fear of exposure led Mark's daughter to finally begin to confide the truth. Her husband was a harsh disciplinarian who, with increasing frequency, spanked their child, slapped him, called him names, and administered humiliating punishments, such as making him stand outside on the porch where neighboring kids could see him. As it turned out, Mark's son-in-law had not caused the bruises Mark saw on the boy—those were the result of a bicycle fall. But Mark's daughter confided that she wouldn't be surprised if the violence were to escalate. She was afraid of her husband.

If she stood up for her son, her husband would put his face close to hers, grab her shoulders tightly, and yell at her, blaming her for "spoiling" the boy. When her husband was out of control, she would make silent plans to get away. But then her husband would return to normal, acting contrite and loving for days or weeks at a time. During the calm periods, he was the ideal husband and father. She began thinking it was up to her and her son to avoid doing things that would "set him off," believing she was somehow to blame. Mark was able to reassure his daughter that she was a wonderful mother, that her son was a good boy, and that her husband was the one with the problem. Once the subject was out in the open, Mark was in a position to guide his daughter toward help.

Addiction

Addiction can take many forms: sex, drugs, shopping, gambling, or overeating. Addicts come in all forms, from poor and uneducated to very bright, well-to-do, and successful people. Addicts are often overwhelmed people who seek respite in an addictive activity so they can be temporarily taken away from their suffering.

If you sense your child is out of control and acting impulsively with money, sex, drugs, or gambling, first decide the magnitude of the problem—how long it has gone on, what is its intensity, how frequently does it arise, and how much does it affect the other aspects of the person's life.

Signs that behavior is destructive include drinking and driving; heavy drinking or drug use, especially while pregnant; making mistakes on the job and ignoring declining health. It's noteworthy when addictive behavior becomes the only focus of entertainment and results in the discontinuation of other activities.

Addictive behaviors can have a biochemical component as well as a psychological aspect and require professional help. Sometimes medication or hospitalization is necessary. Substance abusers may require a detoxification period, which is just the first step of their recovery. Learning to abstain from taking the substance or from participating in the obsessive activity requires tremendous work.

Addicts must learn to create a healthy lifestyle with which to replace their obsession. Often they must change eating, sleeping, recreational habits in addition to giving up the addictive activity. Above all, they must learn to cope with the stress of life without turning to their addictive behavior. Addicts are well-known for lying, breaking promises, and evading responsibility. Their problems will only get worse without intervention.

Being the parent of an addict can be, quite simply, hell. You are up against such a powerful force; some people will willingly give up their jobs, homes, hobbies, families, and even their own children in order to keep their habit. If you can get back to that place of unconditional love in your heart, you may be able to reach the wounded heart of your addicted child. As is often said in twelve-step programs, "Hate the disease, not the person." The first step you need to take is to learn as much as you can about resources such as medical insurance, self-help programs, and treatment sources. Second, get support for yourself. Third, formulate a plan to help you deal with relapses and to stay connected.

Lynn

Lynn learned through reading and conversing with other parents of alcoholics that her son was the type of person who needed structure and schedules. She remembered that he had done his best when he had been in the rigid structure of the military. On his own he became easily disorganized and unable to provide his own structure. At first, she tried to give him the job of remodeling the house, as a way of paying his rent. She thought the work would help him think about his past and future, but instead it gave him too much freedom and also made him feel isolated. His recovery was stalled.

Lynn regrouped, with the help of her Al-Anon support group, and helped her son find a job with an electronics firm where the work was intense and on a predictable schedule. His Alcoholics Anonymous sponsor, who recognized the symptoms of post-traumatic stress disorder typical of Vietnam veterans, stepped in and provided more structure by suggesting some healthy social outlets for him.

Meanwhile, Lynn continued her personal work, coming to further understand that she needed to be more assertive and to remember to express her frustrations and expectations with her son in a healthy way. With time, he began to respond to the authentic way she related to him, and he seemed to grow more relaxed in her presence and in his life.

Psychological Problems

There are many psychological problems that manifest as other problems, including criminal behavior, inability to form relationships, and incompetence in the workplace. If you suspect your adult child has such a problem, you'll need professional guidance immediately to determine what your child's problems might be before you take any action.

Depression is one of the most common psychological disorders. This is a complex disease that takes many forms. Some symptoms might not look like depression but are part of the progression of the disease. A family member who takes notice of behavioral changes can save a loved one's life. Signs of depression are sometimes misinterpreted as character faults rather than as aspects of a psycho-physiological disease. Anyone can become depressed, as it's something that people have no control over and is often genetically based. Sometimes depression is triggered by trauma or loss, but other forms of depression can appear out of the blue. Signs to look for include disturbances in eating and sleeping habits, hygiene practices, memory abilities, and energy levels. Mood swings and indecisiveness can accompany the illness, as well as poor coping with stressors that were previously handled with ease.

If you suspect your child has a problem with depression, make sure there are no weapons in the home. If you fear suicide, talk about it directly, both with your child and with a professional. This is a time to be safe rather than sorry. Sometimes, hospitalization is the only way to keep the depressed person safe and get the illness stabilized, so don't rule this out. It's not giving up to go into an institution for a short while for help. Often, medication can be a tremendous help. Sometimes you have to hang in there while the most beneficial medicine is found for your child. During this time, avoid telling your child how they should be feeling. This is the time to practice the best listening skills you have. If your child is having trouble getting to the doctor, offer to go along to the first appointment.

Connie

Connie was anguished over the possibility that her son suffered from depression. In painfully sad moments, she pictured herself tiptoeing over to his apartment and, while he was sleeping, holding him in her arms and rocking him just like the mother in Robert Munsch's children's book Love You Forever. *Connie wanted to do anything to help her son recover.*

After confronting the history of depression in her own family, she became less passive about her son's problem. She sent away for pamphlets on depression from the National Institute for Mental Health, gave the information to her son, and then asked him to go with her to see a psychiatrist. At first, he insisted he didn't want to take any drugs but agreed to go to the appointment. After talking to the psychiatrist, he became willing to try medication and to embark on therapy. Connie was surprised by how quickly he came around, and wished she hadn't waited so long to do something.

When Is It Just Meddling?

Threats to health and safety are red flags beckoning for your attention. But, as the parent of an adult, you should think carefully about whether to get involved in situations that, while bothersome, are not threatening. It's particularly dicey when you want to intervene in matters such as personal values, lifestyle decisions, and financial decisions that don't involve you personally. You may feel the need to make your opinions known (methods to do this are discussed in chapter 6, "Beyond Advice: Enlightened Communication"), but be careful not to confuse offering opinions and intervening.

Paula

Paula still had her visual aids about the nutrition pyramid, an article about family investments from a business magazine, and a computer program for time management. But, since her return from the women's retreat where she confronted her own problems with perfectionism, she's been focusing on her own life and finds she's no longer desperately driven toward giving advice to her kids. But if they decided to welcome her opinions, she'd be ready.

Don

Don finally talked to the family priest about his daughter's emotional distance from the family. With help from the priest, Don realized that he still had negative judgments about his daughter's lifestyle that would never completely go away. As much as he tried to be accepting, he was worried about two women raising a son without a father.

Don realized that part of his insistence about his daughter coming to visit stemmed from his own desire to have an influence over his grandson and to give him some "normal" family experiences. Without knowing it, Don was trying to intervene in his daughter's life. The priest also helped Don realize that he couldn't change his daughter; he could only change himself and his reactions to her.

Don needed to look at his own self-righteousness, the demands he had placed on his daughter in the past, and the ways in which his judgments were standing in the way of his love. Even if he couldn't change her, he could change himself. Maybe his self-awareness could open the door to a relationship with his new grandson. That would mean so much to his wife, as well as to himself. But to make that happen, Don would have to control his strong desire to exert his influence in his grandson's life.

Anne

Anne realized that her daughter's nagging of her grandson wasn't a life-or-death situation, but it upset her enough that she talked to a therapist about it. Anne remembered that after she had remarried, she had wanted her daughter to "do things right" in order to keep things running smoothly with her new stepfather. Anne was certain that her daughter did not remember how difficult that had been, or she would never have repeated the dysfunctional pattern. When Anne came to realize where her daughter had picked up the habit of nagging, she shared her insights in an environment of mutual trust. Ultimately, her daughter was able to "see" what previously had been unconscious behavior on her part.

Kathryn

The creativity workshop turned out to be a successful venture in many ways for Kathryn and her daughter. She was warmed to see her daughter's eyes light up during a discussion about ways to rekindle the creative spark. After the first day's session, her daughter went to an art store and bought some watercolor paints, just to try out some ideas that had come up. Kathryn sat down to try her hand at writing poetry and was surprised at how the words flowed. But as poetic images formed in Kathryn's mind, she found herself feeling sad, almost depressed, recalling the hollow feelings she had felt early in her own marriage and the similar problems her daughter was facing now. She felt furious with herself for having cheated on her husband years ago and felt furious with her son-in-law for his flirting—and probably worse—with other women. Things were different today. Cheating could result in AIDS.

After the children had gone to bed, Kathryn decided to talk to her daughter about sexually transmitted diseases, hoping she might get the point. Her daughter listened politely, then shook her head. "Mom, I know what you're hinting about, and I don't like it. My marriage is my business and I'm not a fool, okay?" A crackle of anger rose between them and Kathryn worried it might ruin the rest of the weekend. She had spoken too soon, and ungracefully, trying to calm her own fears for her daughter.

Kathryn realized that she could not intervene in her daughter's marriage directly, but she could continue offering her daughter uncon-ditional love and support for her daughter's own personal growth.

Kathryn also decided to share some of her own past struggles with marriage, even though she had decided it was best not to confess to her past infidelities. She was pleased to discover the next morning that her daughter's irritation had passed, and there wasn't a trace of strain between them. By the end of the weekend, her daughter seemed more confident, ready to go to the store back home and get some more art supplies.

When Grown Children Resist Help

Sometimes in our desire to alleviate another's pain or to rescue or cheer up someone, we try to do things against our loved one's will. Unconsciously, we may be trying to substitute our will for that of our children's, which can rob them of the chance to construct their own lives and can serve to demoralize them further.

You don't have the ultimate answer to your child's problem, nor does anyone else. Sometimes your child may feel uncomfortable with the solutions you present, and perhaps their intuition is correct. It's usually counterproductive to try to force your ideas on another person, and you can't always rely on the experts, who may have different opinions about what to do. Maintain an open mind and seek many opinions. Your child is an adult and, regardless of the problem, will have the final say over what happens. If you want to empower someone, you can't dominate them. Offer help on a voluntary basis and avoid a power struggle. If the going gets tough, you'll need to think harder, be more creative, and continue to show your love and affection even if your children choose paths different from the ones you want them to take.

For a parent, any plan of action should aim at giving love and support. Avoid cutting off your own feelings just because it hurts to empathize with a child's suffering. It's tempting to withdraw yourself emotionally at a painful time, but this is when your love is most needed.

When They're Just Having a Hard Time

Sometimes when a grown child is going through a tough transition—whether it be a job loss, a divorce, a time of high stress, an illness, the death of a loved one, a change in their eating or lifestyle habits, or a difficult juncture with their own child-rearing—there may not be anything concrete you can do to relieve their stress.

What you can do is, simply, stay close. There's an age-old comforting question: "What can I do to help?" You can ask your child this question in a way that says you mean it. You can be specific in your offerings, which may be helpful to someone who is too stressed to know what they need. For example, you could suggest practical support, such as going shopping for them, cooking a meal, cleaning their house, helping with paperwork, or providing child care. And you can offer to create a fun diversion for your grandchild, such as bringing over art supplies for an afternoon of making things, going to a movie, or delivering a stack of books.

You can also do research on your own about your child's particular issue. That way, you'll know more, be able to provide more appropriate support, and be able to share the information—when your child is open to receiving it.

Checklist for Intervening

Before you proceed with a plan, ask yourself:

_____ Is this empowering to my grown child?

_____ Am I taking a rational rather than panicked approach?

_____ Have I done my homework?

_____ Am I being kind?

_____ Does my child feel warmth and a sense of belonging when they are with me?

_____ Does my child know that I believe in them?

_____ Am I clear in my own mind about my boundaries?

_____ Can I let my child know I feel honored to be able to help them?

_____ Am I still looking after myself while being strong for my child?

_____ Do I have my support system together?

Unconditional Love

Unconditional love doesn't mean solving someone else's problems or neglecting your own needs. It means coping with your feelings and being willing to support your child, even when things get messy. Unconditional love means avoiding blame. Despite some of the New Age teachings about how people are responsible for everything that happens to them, it seems that much of what occurs to a person is caused by fate, genetics, or other influences far beyond the individual's control. Blaming the individual eclipses compassion and prevents us from seeing the growth that can come out of struggle.

Unconditional love is a gift to your child and to yourself. By staying close to your loved ones during their struggles, you enter into deeper relationships with them, especially if you can develop skills for deeper listening and observing and can develop an appreciation of human limitations. You can once again become an important witness to growth, just as you were when your children were younger and you watched and guided them as they made mistakes and learned their way.

One reason why so many people turn to therapists is because they no longer have deep family connections. Families who are caught up in striving for organization, order, and decorum often will turn away from the kind of attachment that can heal. Sometimes, people want to avoid the complexity and messiness of deep family life, so they fail to blend together. Sometimes, the work of fostering a close family life seems too demanding. Often, families can not bear to be open, vulnerable, and receptive to the human condition—which includes weaknesses, mood swings, irrationality, and foolishness.

It takes patience, time, and authenticity to support another person, especially in a society geared toward immediate gratification. But you can choose to look beneath the surface, accepting the truth of what you see. And through wise contemplation, you'll know when it's time to wait and when it's time to act.

Evaluating Your Plan for Intervention

Before embarking on the decision about whether and how to intervene in the life of your grown child, compare the pros and cons of taking action. Comparing the two sides will help you decide on your course of action.

Exercise

What Could Happen if I Intervene:	What Could Happen if I Do Not Intervene:
_____	_____
_____	_____
_____	_____
_____	_____
_____	_____
_____	_____
_____	_____

_____   _____

_____   _____

_____   _____

Whether or not you take action, you already are behaving coura-
geously by looking squarely at the issue, caring enough to observe and
evaluate your grown child's problem, and admitting your part in the situation. If problems with your child begin to cause you to panic, be sure you
get help for yourself. Sometimes getting involved with social action groups
can provide you with relief through the important contributions they make
to many people in need. Groups such as The Alliance for the Mentally Ill,
Mothers Against Drunk Driving, Women Against Rape, YWCA Shelter Programs, and alcohol and drug treatment centers always need volunteers.
Here you will find people to talk with about the real and pressing issues
affecting you and your family.

While there's nothing anyone can say or do during those dark hours of
the night when you wake up worried and confused, wishing you could
relieve the suffering of someone you love so much, you can take comfort in
knowing you are doing all you can.

Crisis is a part of family life. The question is not "Will you have problems?" but rather "How will you handle them when they come up?" You'd
probably be surprised to discover how many people have coped with serious life problems—their own or those of their family members—at one time
or another. By choosing to be someone who bravely stands by their grown
children as they face tough issues—especially if you are devoted to self-reflection as well as to maintaining a compassionate, realistic view of others—you will earn the trust and inner satisfaction that come from giving real
support. The hard work you put into the parent-child relationship will pay
off by forging strong, enduring bonds. And once the crisis is passed, you
will have all the more reason to cherish the well-deserved good times you
and your child have together.

CHAPTER 9

Enjoying Your Grown Children

Family is a way of holding hands with forever.
—Noah ben Shea

Love doesn't just sit there, like a stone, it has to be made, like bread; remade all the time, made new.
—Ursula K. LeGuin

When your children grow up, it takes creativity to come up with ways to have fun together, enjoy one another's company in a relaxed environment, and celebrate important occasions as a family. The need to remain connected through shared events and celebrations is fundamental. Once people are living separate lives and involved in their own pursuits, they need something to replace day-to-day routines that once provided predictable reinforcers of the familial bond.

When your child was young, you probably had many activities that became rituals, perhaps without your even knowing it. Maybe it was a bedtime prayer or story, a weekly movie, an eccentric way that you celebrated birthdays, or a special restaurant you went to after school functions or sporting events. Most families develop patterns that provide children with a sense of what Dr. Stephen Covey calls the "family culture." In his audiotape "The Seven Habits of Highly Effective Families" (1996), Covey makes an argument for intentionally creating rituals, routines, and events that help children clarify values and see themselves as part of a family system with comfortable, predictable patterns. Kids love to talk about things "we do" that define their families.

After people become separated from their families by geography and by the nature of their busy, independent lives, it can be a challenge to find ways to stay connected—particularly if you want to maintain your relationship with meaningful interactions rather than settling for perfunctory contacts. It's tempting to slide into empty routines in a society that too often emphasizes form over content, materialism over spirituality, and the quick fix rather than the thoughtful actions that keep the family culture alive. However, resisting this "easy way out," many families are discovering new rituals and methods of communication that keep them feeling nestled in familial love—despite the constraints of time and geographic distance. These people are tuned in to the unique personalities within the family, rather than focused on the externally imposed social routines that too often dictate the way extended family members relate to one another.

Obligations

Sometimes we learn to settle for meaningless overtures between the generations as a substitute for genuine connection. Many children dread Mother's Day or Father's Day and feel annoyed by the greeting card ads admonishing them to do something special for their parents. Some parents, in return, strain to figure out the appropriate gifts for children and grandchildren they don't really know well enough anymore to make a suitable selection. It's as much a strain to give as it is to receive gifts or cards when they are delivered out of obligation rather than from a comfortable desire to share or, better yet, an exuberant delight in knowing enough about another person to give something certain to please.

Similarly, the angst of the obligatory family holiday is legendary and is often the source of tragi-comedy. One woman describes her cross-country visits home as her "guilt trips." Many people laugh while watching Chevy Chase in *Christmas Vacation* and cry while watching Holly Hunter in *Home for the Holidays* because most of us have experienced at least one holiday when magnanimous attempts at familial generosity turned from joviality to disaster. Holiday depression is a well-documented condition, and much of it stems from the gap between expectations and reality. On Christmas, the standard for goodness is set by Jesus and Santa Claus, for heaven's sake, and who can live up to that?

No one wants to shower loved ones with "should's." On the other hand, most people want to give and receive loving expressions from their family members. If they retain any connection at all with family, they usually want to be together for at least some of the consequential holidays and events in the family. And, if they are seeking a deeper relationship with family members, they probably want to go beyond the standard times of year for visits and gifts, establishing customs of that allow them to enjoy each other's company at various times throughout the year, while perpetuating the special traditions that define the family.

This is a mobile society, one that requires flexibility, so you need to be innovative in finding rituals that invite willing participation by your children—instead of becoming just another item on their "things to do" list. These well-designed activities can enrich the lives of both you and your children and can become integrated into your family culture. As your grown children create their own family traditions, getting together with their friends and in-laws, it can be a challenge to "fit in" your time with them. This makes it all the more essential to establish some regular traditions that everyone looks forward to, not as an obligation but as a welcome reprieve from daily life.

The Head of the Table

It's a somewhat daunting role for many of us to suddenly find ourselves the matriarch or patriarch of a family, but that's the natural progression after your offspring reach adulthood. You may still be growing and changing yourself, but within your family, you take the place of an elder. Whether or not you provided effective leadership while you were raising your children, you can do so at this phase, creatively taking the responsibility for defining and maintaining the family culture. How you function in this role today depends a lot on what happened in the past. How you handle it in the future is up to you.

Once you have gone through the steps of self-analysis about your past role as a parent, worked to understand your child better, and deepened your level of communication, you should be in a good position to bring meaningful offerings to your immediate and extended family.

Use your imagination. Midlife can be a time to reclaim and harness your own feelings from childhood. You can be daring, flamboyant, and different. This is a time of life to awaken to new possibilities and take action to enrich your own life and those of your family members. The ingredients for creating pleasurable interactions are already there; it's just a matter of packaging them in a way that others will welcome.

Family Traditions

Joyful family experiences from the past can provide inspiration for creating new traditions. Was there a particular place you went often when your kids were young? A kind of food they considered a special treat? A family joke? A popular vacation spot? An activity, such as skiing or badminton, where all of you got into the act? A game that you always played in the car? A children's book that became a favorite? A halcyon moment that your child shared with a grandparent or aunt? A holiday custom that was unique to your family?

Exercise

Take a moment to think about experiences from the past that stand out in your mind as defining moments, times when you said, "Yes, this is our family." Now write them down and, in the process, allow yourself to feel again the emotions you experienced at the time.

I remember

_____

_____

_____

_____

From those ideas, consider the possibility of incorporating past experiences of shared enjoyment into future events. Here are some ways that other parents participated in this exercise.

Michael sent a Dr. Seuss book to his grandchildren with an inscription saying, "I read this to your Daddy when he was little. Now he can read it to you!"

Rosa wrote to her daughter recalling an afternoon when her daughter was about ten. They had camped in the mountains and watched a meteor shower, making wishes on every falling star. Rose described her memories of that event and told her daughter how much she cherished her memories of those times they shared.

When Kathryn's daughter came home for a visit, Kathryn took her to a cafe they used to frequent when her daughter was small, that was still owned by the same couple and that still had the most sinful chocolate shakes on Earth.

When Don and his wife wrote a letter inviting their daughter, her partner, and their son to visit, he suggested getting her cousins and their kids together for a baseball game at the park where they used to go play baseball when the kids were small. With all the grandkids, they'd have more than enough for two teams.

Jake found an old picture of the time he had taken his daughter fishing and she caught her first trout. Fishing was one of the things they

used to do together, when she was small, during his rare days off work.
He sent the picture to her, along with a fishing pole and a
bait-and-tackle box as a Christmas gift.

It's so warming to be able to say, "This is what we do in our family. This is our tradition." Rituals create a sense of stability and often result in the realization that there is a structure in the family. If you're searching for traditions, try talking to people of your parents' generation. What did they do that was special to the family? Where did they go? Even if you didn't bring these traditions into your own home when your children were growing up, it's not too late to tell your kids about their ancestral legacy now.

If you can't come up with traditions from the past, you can invent some. What defines you as a person? Are you an artist? A cook? A gardener? You can pass along whatever you do that seems central to your identity, whether it's your favorite spaghetti sauce or your pen-and-ink drawings of your children and grandchildren.

Exercise

Take a moment to write down what you have to offer. Try to choose things that are particular to your personality and that your children appreciate.

_____

_____

_____

_____

_____

Rituals can provide the opportunity to symbolically link the new generations to their ancestors. It takes time and effort to create rituals and perpetuate them, but the result can be invaluable to you, your children, and grandchildren.

Psychologist Erik Erikson, the author of *Childhood and Society* (1950), studied the phase of life after children are grown and concluded that it is a time when parents can move toward either integrity or despair. People can sink into depression or despair if they begin to feel disconnected from the people and relationships that once defined their lives. Integrity comes with finding meaning in life by renewing love and focusing on personal growth. Guiding the next generation is one way to become integrated, and creating rituals—nourishing ways to be together—can be a powerful symbol of one's commitment to family.

When you choose this integrity, you move beyond obligatory get-to-gethers and phone calls. You put time and energy into improving relationships and creating activities that encourage mutual growth. You look for activities that bring people together and leave them feeling refreshed, with a sense of vitality and belonging. Afterwards, family members can say, "We should do this more often!" even though everyone knows that the competing demands of daily life make it difficult to get together as often as they'd like. As difficult as it is to coordinate events, the effort is worth it, because it provides a way for you and for your children to counteract the rootless, alienated feeling that many people in our society have today. Regular rituals can be particularly comforting during times of transition.

Anne

Anne's family is musically inclined, so singing and playing instruments were a shared source of joy when the kids were growing up. Her family also has a tradition of celebrating "decade" events, so although they don't always get together for every birthday, they try to attend the big birthdays (thirty, forty, etc.) and turn decade anniversaries into special family events. Anne remembers sending her parents a tape of love songs for their fiftieth anniversary. They enjoyed it so much that she decided to make music her "thing" with the kids, and began sending them musical tapes—new recordings she thought they'd like, as well as collections of music they enjoyed in their youth. She began taking time to remember the songs that the kids liked growing up, stringing together Beatles' songs, Bach pieces, Moby Grape, and other unlikely combinations in a single tape. She also decided to make the "decade" celebrations more predictable by planning them way ahead, inviting people months in advance and reminding them to bring their musical instruments.

Kathryn

Many of the people in Kathryn's family enjoy using the Internet. They frequently send one another E-mail messages, sometimes asking the messages to be passed along if they contain details about a particularly momentous occasion. Kathryn decided to take this form of connection to the next level, creating a "chat room" for the family every Sunday evening at eight o'clock. They usually stay on-line together for at least thirty minutes, exchanging jokes, news, and ideas for future get-togethers.

Her daughter, who had embraced her renewed role as an artist, came up with some wild computer graphics she created from keyboard punctuation marks and sent them to her mother over the Internet.

Beth

As Beth began to reflect more upon her awkwardness when it came to emotional issues, memories surfaced about how she and her son had communicated when he was younger. One way they connected was through films. They often went to the movies and especially enjoyed old classics. Afterwards, they would discuss the characters and plots, sometimes expanding the conversation to include their own ideas and feelings. She decided to rekindle those memories and found some postcards with scenes from old movies they had seen together. "Remember this film?" she wrote on the back of a card with a scene from an Alfred Hitchcock suspense movie. "Maybe we'll rent it next time we all get together." She also recalled how much she and her son had enjoyed hiking years ago—long, quiet walks puncuated by relaxed conversation. Beth knew her daughter-in-law loved the outdoors, too. In another letter, she wrote to her son about exploring a new trail she had discovered in one of the rambling state parks near her home. "It would be fun to share it with you two. How about bringing your hiking shoes next time you visit?"

Richard

In Richard's family, the Fourth of July has evolved into the big family holiday. The event started out in the backyard with sparklers twenty years ago, but it's gotten so big that now it's at a park. As the years go by, Richard involves his kids and grandkids more in the production of the main event, a family talent show, getting their help to build a makeshift stage and decorate the area, as well as plan sporting events and contribute to the giant potluck. With the kids' help, frisbee-throwing contests were added to the usual gunnysack races, and each year something new is added.

Paula

Paula is an artist, and over the years she has made many sketches of family members from photographs. She has always been pleased when visiting family members' homes to find the framed sketches prominently displayed. Although her children have other in-laws competing for family members on holidays, Paula decided to make Thanksgiving "her" event each year. She began inviting her kids to bring their in-laws, and created a tradition of taking a family photograph on the steps of her house and then using the photograph to make a sketch of the whole bunch. Everyone who came to the event was included in the sketch. This is now a popular tradition in her family, and family members have come to see Thanksgiving as the holiday to *create a permanent record of how they look from year to year. Everyone wants to "be in the picture."*

Richard

Richard had always been fascinated by genealogy and undertook and investigation into his family's roots. He devoted a wall in his study to a pictorial map of his family's history. On a giant map, he marked the places where his and his wife's ancestors were born and used arrows to show where they moved. He used a copy machine to photocopy old family photographs, which he pasted near their birthplaces. Around the map, he mounted brief stories about the lives of ancestors he had traced, as well as historical information he gleaned about the clothing, architecture, political situations, and other hallmarks of the time. The wall became a focal point of interest for family members and visitors. His grandchildren were especially responsive to the brightly-colored, graphic depiction of their roots.

Mark

Many of Mark's family members live close by, while others live at a distance. Passover dinner has become such a major event that it is unwieldy to have it at one person's home, so Mark instituted the tradition of a "progressive dinner." People who fly in from out of town stay at other family members' homes and help with the course served at that home. That way, out-of-towners get a chance to visit everyone's home and no one has an overwhelming amount of preparation to do.

Sally

Sally's house had boxes full of the things from her kids' childhood, in disorganized stacks in the attic, garage, and outdoor shed. The prospect of going through all the stuff was daunting, until one day Sally's daughter wandered out of the garage with a big grin on her face. "My old platform shoes! Did you know these came back in style?" Suddenly, instead of being the family pack rat, Sally found herself the family historian and museum curator. She'd never imagined that one of her kids would be so pleased to see an old report card from first grade, but they were delighted to see the letter grades and the teacher's comments. Old bedtime storybooks and board games were particular favorites. One son thought she was brilliant to have saved an old metal lunch box that Sally had looked at for years and wondered, "Why in Heaven's name did I keep that?" Now she knew. It was a collector's item. Sorting through boxes, looking at photos, and laughing at memories became a regular feature of family get-togethers until slowly

*the boxes began to disappear. When Sally would visit her children,
they'd inevitably show her anything that was destined for Goodwill or
the trash heap. She'd usually salvage something and they'd laugh,
"For Mom's new collection."*

Tom

*Throughout his academic career, Tom had enjoyed international
literature, art, and foods. Now that he and his wife finally were able to
travel, they cherished the opportunity to become immersed in different
cultures. They collected books, prints, and cookbooks from each country
they visited. In postcards home, they would describe their favorite
meals abroad and their experiences. And when they returned, they
would re-create the dinners for the family, inviting feedback on the
various dishes. They would have a cultural theme for the evening,
sometimes showing a film set in a country they had visited. They
wrote down the recipes that were a hit, along with comments about the
country where they discovered them. They eventually amassed enough
material for a cookbook that also was something of a travelogue, photo
album, and commentary—sometimes with stories or commentaries
Tom had written. Tom photocopied and bound the eclectic collection
and sent copies to his family members.*

Don

*Don has always been a storyteller, a tradition from his Irish
roots. When his kids were small, he would tell them stories about
himself. They especially liked hearing about the times he got in trouble
when he was a kid and how he learned his lessons. Now with his kids
grown, he has made a concerted effort to remember stories about them,
making notes to himself so he won't forget. And now he has
storytelling sessions with their kids.*

Being Original

Every family is different; in some families there may be a deep stoicism, a flair for eccentricity, or a shared rebellious streak that gets in the way of activities that may be viewed as sentimental, hackneyed, or "too much fuss." Then it takes even more creativity to find rituals. Sometimes, however, rituals evolve naturally, with such irresistible integrity that even the most understated person can't help but be moved to continue the tradition.

A sweetly poignant example of this comes from James Clegg, Eileen's husband, whose stiff-upper-lipped British father didn't say too much when, on one Valentine's Day, he received a little dime-store valentine from his then seven-year-old boy. Schooled in understatement, James had written on the back of the valentine simply, "From Jim." One year later, the same valentine appeared. Under "From Jim," his father had written, "From Dad." That same valentine went back and forth for more than forty years, growing worn and tattered as it collected another another addition of the annual shared message, "From Jim," "From Dad," "From Jim. . ." until a few years before his father's death at age ninety-six. James has that precious valentine in a steel box, safely stored as a reminder of a quiet but profound tradition.

It's not a matter of scale but continuity that defines a ritual and provides comfort to both the giver and the receiver. Betty Frain has a developmentally disabled sister who looks forward to correspondence. With the busyness of daily life, Betty has found several shortcuts that make it easier to write to her sister on a regular basis. She picks up postcards whenever she has a chance and has stickers made up with her sister's address. That makes it easy to drop a postcard in the mail at least once a week. She also sends photographs of her family at least once a month. When Betty made the cross-country trip to visit her sister recently, she was moved to see that her sister proudly carries around a purse that's stuffed full of those photos and postcards.

Rituals for Life Transitions

By this time in your life, you have experienced several life transitions and probably realize the importance of each life stage. You also have access to a fair amount of family history that you can share to comfort and provide perspective for family members when they're going through a major life change. Because of your experiences, you are aware of the complexities that come with reaching puberty, giving birth, getting married, moving, getting divorced, going through menopause, getting ill, and experiencing other major life events. Although many cultures and spiritual traditions offer specific activities to support people in getting through these transitions, all too often people recognize the obvious aspects of the event, such as a child being confirmed into a church, without any rituals that place the event in the larger context of the child's first transition into the adult world.

There are both subtle and overt ways to mark these events that can provide great comfort. For a child reaching puberty, one can draw on religious rituals such as Catholic confirmation or Jewish Mitzvahs while also taking time to note the important personal changes that come with reaching the teenage years. Many girls these days are given a celebration party when they have their first menstrual period. Some mothers and fathers mark the occasion with gifts and a visit to the beach, a long walk in the woods, or another activity that involves nature. For girls and boys both, puberty provides an opportunity for parents to talk about sexuality, choices, goals for the future, responsible relationships with the opposite sex, and the beauty of becoming a woman or man. This is also a time when parents and grandparents can encourage grandchildren by together volunteering or doing other community work that will help young children to see and connect with the larger world.

All of life's transitions can become an occasion for sharing and celebration. Housewarmings can become not just an excuse to give and receive gifts but also an initiation of a house into becoming a home. Childbirth can be a time for the parents to receive gifts of photos or writings telling them of their own births. Instead of feeling shunned or abandoned during a divorce, someone recently separated should be able to count on family members to get together and send a gift or plan an occasion to say, "You are still whole; you are not a failure in our eyes." At the onset of menopause, in families that are open to this kind of sharing, humor and shared tales about other family members' experiences help to emphasize the positive aspects of this transition.

Retreats

A relaxing and renewing way to share time with family is a regularly scheduled time together, lasting a few days or even a few weeks, if time permits, at a vacation place. Eileen Clegg, her husband, James, and her son get together with James's grown daughters and their families every year for a weeklong vacation on a beach in North Carolina, renting either a big house or side-by-side condos for a week. Every other year, James's sister, her children, and her grandchildren are part of the event. It's mostly a time for eating; playing tennis, Pictionary, and Trivial Pursuit; getting "Tetris-eyes" in front of the Nintendo; floating in the waves; going to the water slide; and eating some more. But then there are those moments, when everyone else is off playing, and two or three stay behind to have long talks about what's happening in their lives. These magical moments of connection can happen because there is real time to be together in a relaxed environment. They are the most precious of memories, and it's comforting to know that it will happen "same time next year." Annual retreats remind everyone that you're in it for the long haul and that your relationships are forever. It's remarkable to watch the changes from year to year in individual lives. Particularly for children, these annual vacations can become important markers of life's stages and transitions.

Retreats are complicated to arrange, especially if you have a lot of people to assemble. Someone needs to be in charge of choosing a date, reserving a place, and handling the finances. Many families that go on retreats also have a practice of pitching in to help family members who are in tough economic times so that everyone can attend.

As you find yourself in the role of family leader, you may decide to start such a tradition, and you may find yourself arranging it yourself for the first couple of years. But as the tradition becomes popular, others will step in to help with the organization. Be sure to write everything down so you can successfully pass the baton to another family member.

Brainstorming

Spend some time thinking about traditions you'd like to begin. What are the things your loved ones enjoy? What stirs the imagination? You can start with a small act. Here are some thoughts:

- Send favorite poems to loved ones

- Make a family photo album for gifts for special occasions

- Write a journal of your memories and pass it to your child

- Send or give a treat you know your loved ones will like, just to show you are thinking of them

- Send a present that's not for any particular holiday that has personal significance

- Share humor through cartoon books or comedy tapes

- Keep a file of places you'd like to go with family members

- Go to a bookstore or library together

- Volunteer together, choosing an organization or activity that allows you to share your combined talents and interests

- Donation to a charity in the name of a family member

- Fly a kite, roller blade, walk, or take a bicycle trip together

- Plant things together

- Share recipes

- Give plants

- Feed the birds

- Organize a retreat for a long weekend

- Rent motel rooms near an adult child who is feeling isolated, giving family members a place to swim and play together

- Invite family members to go together to a place of worship, and have a luncheon afterward

- Hike at a nearby park that you haven't yet explored

Exercise

Now come up with a list of your own ideas, and share it with your family.

_____

_____

_____

_____

_____

_____

_____

_____

_____

There's joy in a great family meal or sitting in a circle around a child who is gleefully opening birthday presents, but it's enriching for everyone to find new and different venues for family gatherings. Many families revive and carry on old family traditions through outings, games, sports, and other activities that have been enjoyed through the generations. There's a brightening that comes into the faces of young ones when they realize they're doing something that their own parents did as children. It's a similar look that comes to the faces of grandparents when they discover that an old-fashioned wooden toy brings the same joy to a child today as it did for them in their youth. Searching for new ways to connect people through play is a joy in itself. And what greater gift is there for grown children—caught up as they are in the busyness of life—than a few time-tested recipes for fun?

CHAPTER 10

Coming up with Your Strategy

Those who love deeply never grow old.

—Sir Arthur Wing Pinero

When you understand, you love. And when you love, you naturally act in a way that can relieve the suffering of people.

—Thich Nhat Hanh, *Being Peace*

In architecture, there is a concept called the "critical path"—it's a process that enables a designer to take steps to create a building, while regularly evaluating and re-evaluating what's working and what isn't working along the way. The assumption behind this concept is that there will be some false starts, steps backwards, and regrouping before the final plans takes shape. This same idea is a good metaphor for creating a new path in a relationship.

In the beginning of this book, you were asked to identify a specific issue that you wanted to address in relation to your grown child. Perhaps you expected, or hoped, that a solution existed somewhere "out there" and believed it was just a matter of locating it. Perhaps, instead, you have discovered that there is no external set of rules to follow; you can rely on your internal knowledge, gained through self-reflection and an honest analysis of your relationship with your grown child. That can guide you along a path that will evolve, taking you to new places within your own heart and the heart of your family.

Now you can take stock of those resources and use them to make an articulate plan for the future. Go back and review your notes, insights, and thoughts that you recorded throughout this workbook. Be open to the graceful metamorphoses that can occur if you let go of rigid expectations and acknowledge that there is no blueprint but a certain amount of mystery in the process.

Exercise

Ask yourself these questions, which are similar to those posed earlier in the book, but may have different answers now that you have taken a self-reflective journey.

1. What is the primary issue I'm now dealing with in relation to my grown child?

_____

_____

_____

2. What is "my part" to play in resolving or dealing with the issue?

_____

_____

_____

3. Do I need additional resources? If so, what?

_____

_____

_____

4. What do I have to communicate to my child?

_____

_____

_____

5. How and when will I communicate it?

_____

_____

_____

6. What response do I envision?

_____

_____

_____

7. If I don't get that response, what is my next step?

_____

_____

_____

8. How will I continue if I do not get the desired response from my grown child?

_____

_____

_____

9. How am I nurturing myself independent of the outcome of the issue with my child?

_____

_____

_____

10. What is the greatest gift I could give to my grown child now?

_____

_____

_____

11. What is the most important aspect of our family system affecting my child's life and how can I share that information with my child?

_____

_____

_____

12. What is the clearest way to communicate my love in a way that is not attached to any particular outcome?

_____

_____

_____

Here is how the journey changed for the people whose stories are told in this book:

Anne

Anne's emotional reaction to her daughter's nagging of Anne's grandson changed from feeling upset at her daughter to empathizing with her daughter's frustration. Her daughter's harshness reminded Anne of her own shortcomings as a parent. There was a time when Anne had to let her own daughter down, holding overly high expectations of her to please her new husband. When Anne openly shared her own experiences as a young mother with her daughter, including her mistakes, she enhanced the existing climate of trust in their relationship. Within this atmosphere of warmth, Anne was able to share her observations, and her daughter was able to hear those concerns without feeling defensive. They talked about other ways to provide discipline and teaching and emphasized Anne's belief that patience and humor work best with a young child. Anne's grandson flourished in his more supportive environment, and Anne and her daughter became even closer with that tension resolved.

Michael

Instead of being an outside observer merely judging his son's parenting, Michael made an about-face and decided to give more of himself to his son and grandkids. Michael realized that his austerity probably had contributed to his son's tendency to spoil his own children. He saw the irony in that, while thinking his grandkids were rude, he had been rude himself by inquiring how much his son spent on the children's extravagant wardrobes, sports equipment, and toys. With this new understanding of himself, he began doing more activities with his family. They began cooking and assembling models together, and Michael took them to plays and art museums. He became a role model for emphasizing the importance of relationships over material possessions.

Kathryn

Whenever Kathryn would begin obsessing over her son-in-law's flirtations, she would vent her feelings in writing. Sometimes she would write a letter to him and tear it up. Other times, her fury would fuel a dark piece of poetry. More and more, she began to see how her passion for writing was a way to transform and work through her feelings. It was clear that her daughter had to put up a "Stop" sign to any attempt by Kathryn to offer opinions about the marriage. But Kathryn could see the subtle ways in which her daughter was becoming more confident and strong as her artwork blossomed, gaining some local attention not only from friends in her social circle but also from gallery owners. Kathryn felt as though she had provided her daughter with the best support possible, by helping her daughter see her own talents and strength. Still worried, but knowing at this point there was little more she could do for her daughter, Kathryn turned her attention more and more to her own marriage; with her newfound awareness about what had gone wrong years ago, she had grown more open. More than ever, she appreciated her husband's steadfastness through the years. Kathryn gained more insight into herself, and slowly, she began confiding in her daughter, sharing some of her good memories and regrets. She talked about her emotional absence when her daughter was young. Tears came to Kathryn's eyes when her daughter responded matter-of-factly, "But you're here now, Mom."

Mark

Mark's decision to intervene in his son-in-law's violent behavior proved to be wise. While his son-in-law had not caused the bruises that triggered Mark's initial concern, Mark was ultimately successful in helping his daughter acknowledge that her husband's harsh discipline of her son was abusive. His daughter also acknowledged her husband's ill treatment of her. Mark offered to let his daughter and grandson stay at his home, and also provided her with information about a shelter highly recommended by a therapist Mark had consulted.

With the prospect of losing his wife and son if he didn't change, Mark's son-in-law reluctantly agreed to attend counseling and parenting classes. Mark's daughter decided to give her husband another chance. Mark had to deal with some guilt about waiting so long to take action. He realized that providing support for his daughter and grandson would probably involve a long and painful process with an uncertain outcome. He made a conscious decision to pursue his own interests, rather than obsessing on his daughter's future, while still making himself available to assist her as needed.

Sally

Sally faced the ongoing challenge of separating her own identity and aspirations from those of her daughter. She came to grips with her own embarrassment of her daughter's choice in men and slowly developed a rapport with her daughter that provided her with some insight into her daughter's dreams and visions, which were very different from Sally's. With this new perspective, she began seeing her daughter and her daughter's fiancé for who they were, rather than for who Sally wished they were. She found ways to demonstrate genuine affection and feel pride in their accomplishments. Sally's daughter, in turn, expressed appreciation for her mother's candor about the problems in their relationship and seemed to feel more at ease as a result of the insight her mother shared with her about her childhood.

Paula

A turnabout occurred in Paula's relationships with her grown children. As she began to let go of trying to influence their decisions, and discovered how hard she was to please, her children began to open up. One daughter admitted, "I never thought I could do anything right in your eyes." As Paula acknowledged her own shortcomings, particularly in the area of tolerance, she felt more like a welcome peer in their midst. As it turned out, they had areas of expertise that were helpful to her. She found herself asking for their opinions.

Connie

After she persuaded her son to see a doctor to deal with his depression, Connie realized how heavily her worries about him had weighed on her. After talking with her sister and husband about the history of mental illness in her family, she felt lighter and more at ease in her own life. Although never clinically depressed herself, Connie realized how much she had been affected by the pain of others. The successful intervention with her son resulted in the strengthening of her marriage, as well as a closer relationship with her son. Even before her son began to experience the full benefits of his medication and therapy,

Connie was able to begin letting go of her habit of taking on the unhappiness of others. She and her husband ventured into new activities as a couple, and family gatherings became more relaxed. Her son gradually began to experience some optimism and greater energy. Connie's relationship with him deepened as they no longer focused on "his problem" but shared insights about family dynamics. Their closeness continued after he met a woman and eventually started a family of his own.

Lynn

Lynn continued struggling with her son for some time, as he would make progress in overcoming his addiction only to "slip" and fail to keep his agreements. She confided in a friend, who was also an attorney, and came to grips not only with the damage he was doing to himself but also with the potential for his doing more harm to others, should he continue on the alcoholic's path. She gained resolve from the talk with her attorney friend and for the first time she really faced the potential for serious legal problems, should her son drink and drive. She felt less and less angry as she became increasingly able to assert her limits. And, during his "good" periods, the two of them talked seriously about his childhood and her regrets about the past. In his "bad" periods, he would try to use her guilt to manipulate her, but she was able to stand her ground and not buy into his manipulation.

Lynn confronted her deepest regrets about how her past indulging of her son may have contributed to his "slips." Finally she was able to communicate an ultimatum with such conviction—and he knew it was in his best interest—that he finally was convinced of her resolve. She offered him one last chance but made it clear that this would be it. He seemed to be on course; he stayed in his twelve-step program, continued in school, kept agreements to pay room and board, and seemed to be headed toward better health and autonomy.

Lynn spent more time at her boyfriend's house and they talked of marriage. Her son's attempts to manipulate her decreased as it became clear to him that Lynn had reclaimed her rights to her own privacy and activities. As she did less caregiving, he showed her more courtesy and respect. One night he cooked dinner for her and said he looked forward to having his own place one day soon—and he said he hoped she'd be happy.

Tom

Despite the seemingly "win/win" nature of the arrangement for his daughter to move home while he and his wife traveled, Tom had to deal with his wife's concerns about his daughter's well-being and his other childrens' resentment about her receiving such a cushy arrangement. He had to balance his wife's desire to continue indulging their daughter with his own conviction that their daughter would need an ongoing series of nudges to help her eventually leave the nest. Tom realized that he would have to find ways to assure his daughter of his love—and convince his wife that his love for his daughter was taking a new form—while holding fast to the ground rules for the house-sitting arrangement. Having a family friend involved in mentoring his daughter proved valuable both for monitoring her progress and for reassuring his wife that their daughter could survive without them. When his daughter thanked him for doing so much to help her, he realized she was making progress.

Richard

Richard unraveled his family's complex misunderstanding over care of his grandkids. As it turned out, his son and daughter-in-law had mistakenly—and perhaps conveniently—believed that Richard did not want them to get babysitters outside of the family. Instead of immediately confronting his family directly about feeling burdened by eleventh-hour requests to provide child care, he set up his golf and activity schedule and gave them a copy of his calendar for the month, indicating liberal amounts of time when he would be available, and happy, to have the grandkids over. At first, his son seemed offended, but Richard was eventually able to communicate the importance of his activities and explain how much happier he would be to help them out if he had control over his schedule. He also expressed his confidence in his son and daughter-in-law's ability to find excellent child care. His time with his grandkids became a matter of choice, which resulted in more joyful experiences together—active pastimes such as hiking, going to the beach, and flying kites became the norm. The TV rarely went on when they came over. He bought a set of children's golf clubs and began taking them out to the putting green, envisioning their future games together.

Rosa

Rosa wasn't sure when she'd ever have a "real" conversation with her daughter. After the walk on the beach, she wrote a painfully honest letter to her daughter about her growing awareness of the way she had contributed to the alienation between them over the years. Rosa was disappointed not to get a response but comforted herself with the knowledge that her daughter was doing well in her own life. Rosa had given of herself, in every way she could imagine. Now it would be up to her daughter to decide how to respond. One outcome was that her daughter no longer put Rosa down or made rude remarks. Instead, she *avoided getting together at all. There was no consistent contact between them. But one day, out of the blue, her daughter sent her a goofy card—with a joke about disorganization, a subject they had laughed about over the years. Rosa was delighted. She began sending her daughter notes, pictures, and an occasional gift, always taking the opportunity to remind her daughter that she loved her. Rosa had confidence that the years would bring them closer together and that she would enjoy a relationship with her future grandchildren. The extraordinary effort she had made to understand and heal the relationship with her daughter made Rosa feel stronger and more hopeful in other aspects of her life. She began to find more satisfaction in her other relationships and blossomed in her career.*

Jake

As Jake set out to impress upon his daughter that he had an interesting life of his own—and wanted to be an active member of her family—he began developing a real interest both in hobbies and in his consulting business. It was tempting to slip back into the busyness that had kept him apart from his daughter years ago, but he kept his focus on the family. With time, and regular but studiously unobtrusive visits, he found his daughter increasingly open to discussing the prospect of his moving to the town where she lived. His daughter and son-in-law were impressed by the thoroughness of his financial planning for health care and other eventualities. He was able to convince them that, in wanting to move closer, he wasn't thinking about just himself, as he had in the past, but also about their family.

Beth

The awkwardness of discussing her feelings slightly lessened, and Beth discovered that her special bond with her son was still there. By creating mutually convenient opportunities to get together—such as sharing a meal during business trips—she re-established a one-on-one relationship with him that eventually opened the way to discussing her concern about having a place in his family life. He admitted feeling pulled away from his mother by his wife and said that his first loyalty was to his wife. He also admitted that Beth's reserved manner and seeming tolerance made it easy for them to cancel their plans with her.

Beth talked of her desire to be close to him and to the coming grandchild, and explained that the holidays weren't as important to her as regular contact. She expressed her love and willingness to be flexible so that her daughter-in-law would not feel as imposed upon. Her son grasped the significance of Beth's unprecedented candor and seemed willing to find creative ways to remain connected to her and to include her in his family life. He gave Beth some insight into her daughter-in-law so that Beth could be more effective in building a relationship with her.

It didn't take long for Beth and her son to drift back into the companionable relationship they had shared when he was growing up. And eventually her daughter-in-law became more comfortable with Beth. Beth's invitations to share specific activities proved successful. The three of them turned out to have many shared interests, including classic films and hiking. Beth's daughter-in-law brought a new dimension to their excursions, with an interest in bird-watching. Beth took care to acknowledge her daughter-in-law's expertise and found ways to express—through words and hugs—how much joy the couple brought into her life.

Don

Don realized that "the problem" was not his lesbian daughter's attitude toward family, but his own rigidity. Although he could not completely change his fundamental belief that his definition of a "natural" family was preferable to his daughter's scenario, he was committed to renewing his bond with his daughter and becoming a part of his grandchild's life. He acknowledged and tried to let go of his judgments about how boys should be raised. As he stretched himself to truly accept his daughter's choices, he found himself more open to other people, within his neighborhood and church congregation, whom he had previously written off because they were "different." As he began leaving behind his harsh judgments of others, he grew more aware of his emotions and went through some belated grieving over past experiences, including the difficult times between him and his daughter during her teenage years. He made a trip to California to visit his daughter and her family, and in their conversations he revealed to them some of his insights about his own past rigidity. He also shared his pride in her accomplishments. Her response was overwhelming. She was so grateful for his acceptance and said she wanted her son to have a strong male figure in his life—one with a capacity to be sensitive like her father.

All of these people changed considerably when they began to look for ways to be better parents to their grown children. Many had support from others, though some embarked on the exploration alone. Most found themselves closer to their children, and some established a healthier distance. But all of them—even Rosa, whose relationship with her daughter had yet to change perceptibly—achieved a sense of peace through their commitment to do their best as parents to their adult children. They became better at loving, grew more mature, and developed personal strengths as they stretched to learn more about themselves and their children on a deeper level.

You can take an active part in changing your relationships by demonstrating compassion without meddling. Striving for connection, self-understanding, a deeper awareness of others, and joyful experiences can become a never-ending, ever-changing quest that will continue to bring you unexpected rewards. When you make a commitment, to your family and to yourself, to live a fuller and more self-aware life—with all of the risks, excitement, pain, and hope that self-awareness brings—your grown children naturally can see they have the potential to do the same.

As you follow through on the plans you have outlined in the exercises at the beginning of this chapter, keeping in mind your backup plan, remember:

- To say with sincerity, "I'm here for you."

- To be specific in your offerings of help.

- To keep in mind that whatever happens to one family member affects the others. As you grow, they will too.

- That everyone's experience is unique.

- That listening is more important than talking.

- That what you do is more important than what you say.

- That there is almost no hurt from the past that will not be lessened by acknowledgment and atonement.

- That taking care of yourself and enjoying your life is not good just for you, but benefits your whole family.

- That there are endless ways to make loving overtures, to say "I'm thinking about you," without intruding.

There is mystery ahead. You can't predict what will happen when you try a new way of communicating with your grown child or when you evolve a new way of understanding yourself.

As you feel more free to be yourself, you'll come to appreciate your grown child in ways you never expected. You'll grow less concerned about big changes and more open to the small pleasures and deep connections that occur in an atmosphere of mutual acceptance.

When you allow yourself to venture forth into uncharted territory— the emotional places where there are more questions than answers—trust that your love will guide you. Ultimately, it is not the imagined "end result," but the path itself that proves to be the treasure. Sharing this wisdom may prove to be the most valuable legacy you will leave for your children.

Organizations That Can Help

Depression

National Alliance for the Mentally Ill
 200 North Glebe Road, Suite 1015
 Arlington, VA 22203-3754
 (703) 524-7600

National Mental Health Association
 1-800-336-1114

Homosexuality

Federation of Parents and Friends of Lesbians and Gays
 1101 14th Street NW, Suite 1030
 Washington, DC 20005
 (202) 638-4200

Abusive Men

Ending Men's Violence Task Group c/o RAVEN
 (314) 645-2075

Child Abuse

Child-Help U.S.A. Child Abuse
  P.O. Box 630
  Los Angeles, CA 90028
  Hotline: 1-800-422-4453

Child Protective Services (listed under county agencies in the phone book)

Domestic Violence

National Coalition Against Domestic Violence
  Business Office: (303) 839-1852
  Hotline: 1-800-799-7233

Your police or sheriff's department

Drugs and Alcoholism

American Council for Drug Education
  164 West 74th Street
  New York, NY 10023
  1-800-488-DRUG

Alcoholic Anonymous (local phone book)

State and county agencies (local phone book)

Cancer

American Cancer Society, Inc.
  2200 Lake Boulevard
  Atlanta, GA 30319
  (404) 816-7800

Legal Information

American Bar Association
  750 N. Lake Shore Drive
  Chicago, IL 60611
  (312) 988-5000

Grandparents

American Association for Retired People/Grandparent Information Center
  AARP Headquarters
  601 E Street NW
  Washington, DC 20049
  (202) 434-2277

Grandparents as Parents (GAP)
  P.O. Box 964
  Lakewood, CA 90714
  (562) 924-3996

References and Resources

Adams, Jane. 1995. *I'm Still Your Mother: How to Get along with Your Grown-up Children for the Rest of Your Life.* New York: Delta.

Baker, Russell. 1983. *Growing Up.* New York: New American Library-Dutton.

Barnes, Christine. "90's Family: The Ultimate Road Trip: Traveling with Adult Kids," *Los Angeles Times,* December 27, 1995.

ben Shea, Noah. "Noah's Window," *Santa Barbara News Press,* December 22, 1996.

Buhler, Charlotte, and Fred Massarick. 1968. *The Course of Human Life.* New York: Springer.

Campbell, Susan. 1984. *Beyond the Power Struggle.* San Luis Obispo, CA: Impact Publishers.

Casey, Karen. 1991. *Each Day a New Beginning.* Center City, MN: Hazelden.

Covey, Stephen. 1996. *The Seven Habits of Highly Effective Families* (audiotapes). Provo, UT: Covey Leadership Center, Inc.

Dass, Ram, and Mirabai Bush. 1992. *Compassion in Action.* New York: Bell Tower.

DeToledo, Sylvie, and Deborah Brown. 1995. *Grandparents as Parents.* New York: Guilford Publications.

Eddy, Peggy, and Leslie Dashew. 1995. "Sorting out What's 'Equal' and What's 'Fair' (Financial Relationships between Parents and Adult Children)." *Nation's Business,* August, 83:8.

Erikson, Erik. 1950. *Childhood and Society.* New York: W. W. Norton.

Estess, Patricia Schiff. 1994. "When Kids Don't Leave: How to Cope with Our Stay-at-Home Offspring." *Modern Maturity* (Nov/Dec).

Evans, Christine Brautigam. 1994. *Breaking Free of the Shame Trap: How Women Get into It, How Women Get out of It.* New York: Ballantine.

Fanning, Patrick, and Matthew McKay. 1987. *Self-Esteem: A Proven Program of Cognitive Techniques for Assessing, Improving, and Maintaining Your Self-Esteem*. Oakland, CA: New Harbinger Publications.

Framo, James L. 1992. *Family of Origin Therapy: An Intergenerational Approach*. New York: Brunner-Mazel.

Fromm, Erich. 1956. *The Art of Loving*. New York: Harper and Brothers.

Funk, Wilfred. 1950. *Word Origins: An Exploration and History of Words and Language*. New York: Wings Books (div. of Random House).

Gould, Roger L. 1972. "The Phases of Life: A Study in Developmental Psychology." *American Journal of Psychiatry* 129:5.

Hendricks, Gay, and Kathlyn Hendricks. 1990. *Conscious Loving: The Journey to Co-Commitment*. New York: Bantam.

Jung, Carl G. 1957. *The Undiscovered Self*. New York: Mentor.

Keirsey, David, and Marilyn Bates. 1984. *Please Understand Me*. Del Mar, CA: Prometheus Nemesis.

Kierkegaard, Søren. 1967. *Journals and Papers*, Vol. 1, edited by Howard V. Hong and Edna H. Hong. Bloomington: Indiana University Press.

Kramer, Jeanette R. 1985. *Family Interfaces: Transgenerational Patterns*. New York: Brunner/Mazel.

Livesley, John. 1966. "Heritability of the Five Personality Dimensions and Their Facets." *Journal of Personality* Vol. 64(3).

McGovern, George. 1996. *Terry: My Daughter's Life and Death Struggle with Alcohol*. New York: Villard.

Munsch, Robert. 1945. *Love You Forever*. Illustrated by Sheila McGraw. Ontario: Firefly Books, Ltd.

Neugarten, Bernice. 1968. *Middle Age and Aging*. Chicago: University of Chicago Press.

Nhat Hanh, Thich. 1987. *Being Peace*. Berkeley: Parallax.

Niles, Bo. 1996. "Home Again: When a Son Moves Back in, the Notion of Family Is Reevaluated." *Country Living*, August.

O'Gormand, Patricia, and Philip Oliver-Diaz. *Breaking the Cycle of Addiction*. Pompano Beach, FL: Health Communications.

Satir, Virginia. 1972. *Peoplemaking*. Palo Alto, CA: Science and Behavioral Books, Inc.

Shakespeare, William. 1984. "The Tragedy of Hamlet, Prince of Denmark." In *The Cambridge Text of the Complete Works of William Shakespeare*. London: Octopus Books, Ltd.

Sheehy, Gail. 1977. *Passages*. New York: Bantam.

_____. 1995. *New Passages: Mapping Your Life across Time*. New York: Ballantine.

Siegel, Bernie. 1997. *News Press*, February 9, 1997.

Sumrall, Amber Coverdale. 1990. *Write to the Heart: Wit and Wisdom of Women Writers*. Freedom, CA: The Crossing Press.

Tinney, Hope Belli. "Sibling Rivalry," *Santa Rosa Press Democrat*, May 21, 1996.

Tulku, Tarthang. 1977. *Gesture of Balance*. Emeryville, CA: Dharma Publishing.

Turnbull, Colin M. 1961. *The Forest People*. New York: Simon and Schuster.

Voirst, Judith. 1986. *Necessary Losses*. New York: Fawcett Gold Medal.

Warner, Carolyn. 1992. *The Last Word: A Treasury of Women's Quotes*. Englewood Cliffs, NJ: Prentice Hall.

Warner, Rex. 1967. *The Stories of the Greeks*. New York: Farrar, Straus, and Giroux.

Index

Acknowledgments

The authors wish to thank publisher Patrick Fanning of New Harbinger Publications for his encouragement that resulted in this book, to editor Kristin Beck for the perspective that broadened the concept, and to editors, Angela Watrous and Kayla Sussell for the care and insight that clarified and deepened the work. Appreciation also goes to the expert skills of librarian Marie McKenzie for her creative research; Gail Vann for her thoughtful input at a critical juncture; and above all, to the many people whose life experiences showed us the possibilities for mending and celebrating intergenerational family ties.

On the personal front:

From Betty: Thanks to my parents for the gift of life. To my dad for his curiosity about the life span and child development in particular, to my mom for her perseverance through many difficult transitions—she is a role model of endurance and strength. My deep gratitude to my children, Sylvia and Michael; may they be rewarded for their good humor, patience, and willingness to do without as I pursued this project. I am indebted to my teachers at Pacific Oaks College, Pasadena, CA, Antioch College, Willow Springs, OH, and Fielding Institute, Santa Barbara, CA for their emphasis on family systems, attachment theories, and adult development. I'm grateful for my work with Dr. Dane Prugh at the University of Colorado Health Sciences Center, as well as with Adele Rosenbaum at Head Start in New York City, where I learned further about individual, social, cultural, and family dynamics. Deep gratitude goes to Bob Gutlaben of the Covenant

Connection, Robin Bowen of California Parenting Institute, Eileen Cummings with her Magical Child Retreats, and Betty Ann Judah of the Dyslexia Center for their inspiration and teachings. Special thanks to my family of choice, Cheryl Jern and Ken Miller, as well as to Lia and Nelson Lee and their children—both families were a special source of comfort and love. I am indebted to the families and interns with whom I had the privilege of working in my private psychotherapy practice. I have been enriched by being a witness to their growth and development. I have also been enriched by and have appreciated the ongoing support of Corinne Heald, Maureen Kampten, Connie Peabody, Carla and Ron Riffel, Larry Safford, and Kathryn Wilson.

From Eileen: I am ever grateful to my husband, James, for his steadfast love and thoughtful nature, and to my son, Justin, for his caring spirit and wild sense of humor. Thanks to both for tolerance when our home was transformed into a paper-strewn nest where the work could thrive. To my friends (you know who you are) for recognizing just when to insist upon walks on the beach and other distractions. Thank you, too, to my stepdaughters, Elizabeth Myles, Susan Wilkes, and Cynthia Clegg (I wish I could claim some credit for the wonderful women you are); to my father, C. David Conn, and mother, Iris Ridgway, (wise parents, both); to my uncle and mentor Roger Ridgway; to my sisters Marsha Siner and Sheila Conn; to my brother Christopher Conn, to the generation we are raising, and to the three generations of elders who taught us about commitment to family: No matter how dramatic the ups and downs, we will always love and belong to one another.

More New Harbinger Titles for Parents and Families

The Ten Things Every Parent Needs to Know
A Guide for New Parents and Everyone Else Who Cares About Children

This engaging and easy-to-use guide offers support and practical counsel for men and women who are becoming parents for the first time or need help dealing with the responsibilities of parenting.

Item KNOW Paperback, $12.95

Kid Cooperation
How to Stop Yelling, Nagging, and Pleading and Get Kids to Cooperate

There really is a way to talk so that kids will listen and be reinforced to be helping, responsive members of the family. This is an empowering work, filled with practical skills.

Item COOP Paperback, $13.95

Why Children Misbehave
And What to Do About It

This text offers practical strategies for dealing with common behavior problems in a concise, easy-to-use format. Beautifully illustrated by over 100 photographs.

Item BEHV Paperback, $14.95

When Anger Hurts Your Kids
A Parent's Guide

Learn how to combat the mistaken beliefs that fuel anger and how to practice the art of problem-solving communication—skills that will let you feel more effective as a parent and let your kids grow up free of anger's damaging effects.

Item HURT Paperback, $12.95

The Power of Two
Secrets to a Strong & Loving Marriage

Details the skills that happy couples use to make decisions together, resolve conflicts, recover after upsets, and convert difficulties into opportunities for growth.

Item PWR Paperback, $13.95

Illuminating the Heart
Steps Toward a More Spiritual Marriage

Outlines steps that couples can take to examine fundamental beliefs, search for shared meaning and purpose, and reconnect to each other, their families, and the wider community.

Item LUM Paperback, $13.95

Call **toll-free 1-800-748-6273** to order. Have your Visa or Mastercard number ready. Or send a check for the titles you want to New Harbinger Publications, 5674 Shattuck Avenue, Oakland, CA 94609. Include $3.80 for the first book and 75¢ for each additional book to cover shipping and handling. (California residents please include appropriate sales tax.) Allow four to six weeks for delivery.

Prices subject to change without notice.